The Redwood

Review

Compliments of the
Third Thursday Writers' Group
Newport, Rhode Island

Volume I	Number 1

Summer 2002

IN MEMORIAM

Jean George

About the Review

www.timshelarts.com/redwoodreview

The Redwood Review is a showcase for the work of the Third Thursday Writers' Group, which meets at 6 p.m. on the third Thursday of every month at the Redwood Library & Athenæum.

In the spirit of open dialogue — and for the love of our craft — we welcome comments regarding individual works or authors or the review as a whole. Send compliments or constructive criticism either to the address below or through the Web site above. Organizations that would like to host public readings from the review are also encouraged to contact the writers' group.

Copies of this periodical are available for free at various locations in the area of Newport, RI. To make a donation toward the next edition or to order copies ($5 each including shipping), send a check or money order, payable to *Timshel Arts,* to the address below or visit our Web site with a credit card in hand.

We would like to thank Susan Ryan for the leadership that she provides at each of our meetings. Our group would not be the success that it is without her involvement. We also thank the staff of the Redwood Library for hosting our meetings and for not throwing books at us when we run a little late.

Published by
Timshel Literature
P.O. Box 751
Portsmouth, RI 02871
www.timshelarts.com

© 2002 by Timshel Literature
All rights reserved
Printed in the United States of America in 2002

ISBN 0-9708317-1-4
Library of Congress Control Number: 2002104541

Table of Contents

By the Sea   1

On the Mainland   47

In a Dream   87

Poetry

Ingrid Mathews
Born on the Cadence 24

Janette van de Geest Van Gruisen
Numb 42

B.E. Delaplain
Elsewhere 44

Gary Bolstridge
Vituperative 52

Ingrid Mathews
Life Grows Richer Still 134

Fiction

Justin Katz
from *A Whispering Through the Branches* 5

Christine L. Mullen
Granda 37

Table of Contents

Lori Dillman
from *The Congregation* 39

A. Valentine Smith
from *A Circle of Three* 43

Janette van de Geest Van Gruisen
from *Pedestrian Crossing, A Novel* 49

Andrew McNabb
A The Bronwyn *Tale* 55

Zona Douthit
Battles & Wars 61

Christine L. Mullen
The Maypole 71

Gary Bolstridge
Dragons 89

A. Valentine Smith
from *At First You See It... . .* 91

Bill Goetzinger
from *The Toonijuk* 95

Gary Bolstridge
Sweet Blood 125

A. Valentine Smith
from *A Circle of Two* 131

Nonfiction

Gary Bolstridge
The Plane Ride 3

Len DeAngelis
Are Adults Too Old for Young Adult Literature? 25

Gary Bolstridge
I-Roc, Do You? 53

Anne DuBose Joslin
from *Dishonorable Intentions* 65

Len DeAngelis
Review: *The Noonday Demon: An Atlas of Depression* 73

Gary Bolstridge
The Rider 83

Photographs

Melissa Martin Ellis
Reflection ....Cover

Justin Katz
Looking Over 1

Ingrid Mathews
Born on the Cadence 24

Melissa Martin Ellis
Shadows 47

Gary Bolstridge
Satyr 87

Gary Bolstridge
Dragon 90

Ingrid Mathews
Life Grows Richer Still 135

Justin Katz

By the Sea

3
The Plane Ride
Gary Bolstridge

5
from *A Whispering
Through the Branches*
Justin Katz

24
Born on the Cadence
Ingrid Mathews

25
*Are Adults Too Old for
Young Adult Literature?*
Len DeAngelis

37
Granda
Christine L. Mullen

39
from *The Congregation*
Lori Dillman

42
Numb
Janette van de Geest
Van Gruisen

43
from *A Circle of Three*
A. Valentine Smith

44
Elsewhere
B.E. Delaplain

The Plane Ride

Gary Bolstridge

We had been circling on the runway of the airport terminal like a car on the beltway around a major city. After an eternity (actually, it was just half an hour) the pilot finally announced that we were cleared for take-off. He explained that our delay had been due to a problem with one of the engines. But, he said, it had fixed itself. That's just what I wanted to hear. Mercifully, the engine(s) carried us into the skies without further mishap.

On board the plane were the two Hide sisters — Leather and Calf. One had skin tougher than the other. Neither wore make-up; their short, sun-bleached blond hair looked as if it had been shorn with sharp rocks. Plain tee-shirts, khaki shorts, white socks, and Timberland boots announced they were hiking through life, scaling obstacles but never stopping to smell the sweetness of pleasure. Mountains, rocks, streams — in fact, all of nature — were acknowledged only when they were defeated in battles of supremacy. Enjoyment was found in perseverance. Their backpacks, safely stowed above, contained enough trail mix to traverse the Cascade Mountain Range. They immediately fell asleep, heads resting on each other, reinforcing their bond, replenishing their strength for the next course of impediments.

Also on board was the health-food nut seated next to me, who had ordered a special meal for the flight. He was downing a concoction of Gelfling essence and fruit. His body, purged of fat and toxins, was in stark contrast to the sweet taffy that bloated his mind. He had purged his body of bad medical test result numbers but had filled his head with the useless numbers of baseball statistics. His body had the look of a marathon runner, sleek and thin. Indeed, he had participated in a couple of Boston marathons, but more importantly — to him — he had run the 100 or so races in his head. Replayed his non-participation and the triumph of others over and over. He tried to infect me with the dribble that he called thought about baseball heroes and their numbers. Fortunately, the flight was soon over, saving me from the purgatory of the banal.

Unfortunately, he showed up on my connecting flight! Not wanting to be subjected to his particular confections, I started coughing uncontrollably in the direction of the empty seat next to me, not covering my mouth, just as he approached. It worked. Rather than occupying the now infected chair, he turned his head from me, an invisible surgeon's mask covering his face to ward off any germs, and continued walking down the aisle.

Just after he passed by me, an older, obese man, wheezing heavily, the audible sound of phlegm in his lungs, collapsed into the space next to me. He completely filled his seat and was inching into mine as he strained to fit his bulk in the confined space. Once berthed in his/my seat, he turned his attention to me. A smile revealed a row of missing teeth (the others yellow from tobacco stain), ready to bore me with the details of his maladies. He immediately coughed a great round of sputum, making loud noises of dismissal.

"Are you alright?" I signed to him, in my own made-up pantomime.

He looked puzzled. I raised the palms of my hands to my ears and garbled a barely decipherable "Can't hear."

He frowned then turned to the person on the other side of the aisle and inflicted the conversation that I would have suffered.

I was left in peace to gaze out the window toward a view of Middle America's nature, cut up and squared off by squares who fight over possession rights. Occasionally, a diagonal cut across the grid, causing anxiety over the boundaries that should have been clearly delineated.

When these battles are won, the reward of personal gratification induces the contentment of inner calm. I could now go to sleep and relax in the thought of my fate, dependent on man's machines and their reliability to lift me to new destinations.

from A Whispering Through the Branches

Justin Katz

Nathaniel was always amazed when they found *their place* in the city. Providence was a maze because it was a city rebuilding. And though Nathaniel, as a rule, preferred the image of cities falling into ruin from disuse, he could not escape the reality that there were opportunities to indulge in culture that the bucolic areas could only provide in small, amateur doses to the extent that they did at all. Ideal, to his way of thinking, would have been the reinstatement of the arts seeping into the country in search of audiences as it had been when the only entertainment, other than the Bible, that was offered to farmers and artisans was the occasional traveling show: minstrels, acting troops, and the grander but less artistic fairs and circuses (which, even though he knew he romanticized them, seemed to have been less ostentatious, but perhaps more authentic for their touch of darkness).

But Nathaniel realized that, for this ideal to become the custom, the artists of the world would have to return to the tradition of either utilizing their particular talents for their own sakes, in which case merely performing is the object and any available crowd, wherever it might be gathered, is as good as another, or to the idea that they were on a mission of some kind, whether educational or proselytic in nature; so he and his wife-to-be had found for themselves a restaurant, though few really went there to eat, that answered both Nathaniel's longing to see the reign of cities decaying and his need for culture because the restaurant (more properly called a bar) was host to jazz musicians, folk singers, spoken wordists, and any other performer whom the clientele might fancy on the ground floor of an otherwise unoccupied, crumbling factory building. Nathaniel himself played there on occasion in the Winter months, less now than when he had made his go at stardom through other methods than he had recently stumbled upon.

This being the case, the owner, the waiters, and a good number of the regular patrons knew him at sight, if not by name, and welcomed him with smiles and pleas for him to play. Often he would hop onto the stage and sit at the old and furrowed, and always appealingly out of tune, piano while the hired band of the evening relaxed for a time among the audience and then drifted back to their instruments and joined him.

On this evening on the cusp of Autumn, with Summer still beating through the open windows and the door, Nathaniel and his fiancé walked into the bar while the band was already away from the stage and indistinguishable in the crowd. Hands clapped Nathaniel on the back while their counterparts waved and pointed toward the stage. Nathaniel gave Jen a look of feigned reluctance, and she swished both hands at the piano with a laugh. Smiling demurely, Nathaniel kissed her and plunged into the throng of bodies. People looked at him and made way, some vaguely acknowledging him with nods, others sensing the general recognition. Jen spotted a friend and slipped through a break in the swarm.

Nathaniel stroked the keys of the piano lightly at first, recalling the piano's feel and personality. His playing was aimless and subtle, barely audible over the collected murmurs around him. Some of the people who had been pressed toward the stage paused in their conversations to ascertain whether the faint music was merely some indistinct reminiscence that only they could hear. As more eyes picked him out and lingered on him, Nathaniel felt the recrudescence of the old habits of euphoria and expanded his melodies, striking them out of the piano more forcefully. Talkers began to refer to him, *who is he?*, and nod, *oh yeah*. Heads could be seen floating toward him through the crowd. He settled on an idea and secured it, beating out the rhythm in chords with his left hand. Then he broke it apart in the melody and in the rhythm and brought it back, and unraveled it into simplicity and threw it open toward commotion. And the heads nodded. He skipped the rhythm of the pattern tritely and somebody laughed. He slowed and raced, finally bringing it down even and low with spurts of broken rhythm. He smiled at the drummer, who was taking up his sticks, because he knew him, and they both took it on, hands together then clashing. Nathaniel softened and the drummer picked it up and took it out then back and Nathaniel went up high when the bass bellowed in. And the bass player winked and took off, with Nathaniel chasing after him and the drummer holding them together. Then a saxophone growled on top from out of nowhere, and Nathaniel looked to see the blower but only saw his back. And he was quick and full of life. Then hurled out a line and it came back, and he returned it upside-down and it was changed and kept going when he picked it up again, and the two instruments beat it out against each other and in harmony and the drummer gave it up and smacked wildly at his drums while the bass groaned out long improbable sighs and the horn screeched and the piano crashed out walls of chords and nonsense runs. Then suddenly, everything was silent and the crowd was mute and breathless. A drop of sweat dripped from Nathaniel's nose, and when it hit the keyboard his original idea burst out of every instrument in unanimity and stopped.

⸲ The crowd roared. Nathaniel stood and smiled. He passed a secret signal to Jen, who had joined her friend at a table. He nodded elatedly at the drummer and smacked the bass player on the back and looked toward the flash of the saxophone, which was raised in acknowledgement of the applause. The horn player turned, and Nathaniel saw that it was Sal.

"Mr. Nathaniel Ariss on the keys," Sal announced, pointing his sax at Nathaniel. "Piano player and author extraordinaire!"

And with that, Sal put his horn to his lips and signaled the band to swing into the next tune. Nathaniel, not sure what should be his response gave a final wave of his arm and hopped off the stage. Jen was sitting with a group of people whom he knew only slightly. They all complimented his performance.

"That was great, honey," Jen told him, asking, "have you played with all of them before?"

Without thought, Nathaniel responded, "All but the sax player," not knowing why he lied.

"Oh," said Jen, looking a little bemused. "How did he know your name?"

"I don't know."

Jen gave it some thought. "I guess he's read your book, and somebody must have pointed you out," she reasoned.

"Maybe," Nathaniel told her, relieved to escape the need to lie further but more than a little concerned that it had been his first impulse to deceive. Then the evening out came on suddenly and its opening scene was all but forgotten by everyone but Nathaniel, who kept it circulating in his mind despite the waves of music from the stage and the onslaught of people who wanted to compliment his piano playing or congratulate him on his having published a book; he suspected that none of these latter had actually read it, as evinced by their offering no evidence either way. Even his increasingly boisterous companions at the table were unable to divert his attention from the impassive figure on the stage who, whether burning up or lulling the keys of his saxophone, gave no sign of zeal or strain behind his sunglasses. *This is too random to be random,* thought Nathaniel.

When the band left the stage for another break, several people pushed through the crowd with a stagger in their step and urged Nathaniel to fill the gap at the piano. The suggestion was taken up by those at his table and nearly took the force of a chant, but Nathaniel blushed and smiled and kindly refused. He was still bothered by the man with whom he had spent more time than any of those around him but his fiancé and who lingered on the edge of his vision until it was time for the final round of music to begin. There had to be something going on, Nathaniel reasoned, or else Sal would have come over to speak with him, even if under the guise of a stranger.

Distracted though he was, through the resumption of the jazz and the pulse of conversation and life and the occasional hush of the audience as the band swept into realms of virtuosity and ingenuity that bordered on brilliancy and the bells for last call and the push of the crowd to the bar and the ripple of inebriated laughter that floated the atmosphere all around him, Nathaniel still turned over and over in his mind his possible actions. Then, suddenly, it was out of his hands because the crowd, without his noticing, dissipated as if it had been half populated by figments of his imagination, and his table was emptied. As the final note was played and the final cue that the show was over was given by the slight reverberation of the instruments as they were laid down, Jen excused herself to the ladies room, and Sal, more ghostlike than even the now evaporated audience, stood before him.

"How's it goin', Nathaniel?" the specter asked.

Stammering, Nathaniel responded, "Fine. Just fine. How about with you?"

Sal shrugged and pulled back his lips in an ambiguous line, and Nathaniel saw his eyebrows peak over the edge of the glasses. "Could be worse, could be better."

Giving an unimportant rejoinder, Nathaniel fell into silence. The drummer came over to tell Sal that it had been a lot of fun playing with him and said goodnight to Nathaniel. Nathaniel turned to Sal when the drummer had gone, "So what brings you to Providence?"

Nonchalantly, Sal told him, "I've been looking for you."

"Oh?"

"Yeah, the bio in your book only said Rhode Island, so I figured I'd catch up with you if I played around Providence for a while."

"Have you been around long?"

"Not long."

Seeing that Sal was not going to offer up his intentions without being prompted, Nathaniel asked, "So, why were you looking for me?"

As if this question had been some cue in a script to which Nathaniel had not been privy, Sal flung himself into a chair at the table. "You've been havin' some success with that book of yours, haven't you?"

Nathaniel spoke cautiously, "I suppose so. Did you read it?"

"Yeah, some of it. Listen, what I'm wonderin's if you could help me slip into the big time."

"I don't know what you mean."

"Aw, come on, we both know that when yer in, yer in. I just need some help getting a shot. All you'd have to do is introduce me to some people or get me a gig at some party where there are important people. Or maybe you could just bring some of your literary friends to see me. Man, I'm good, I just need some exposure."

Nathaniel wasn't sure what he could do. "I know you're good... really good, but I don't have many friends period, let alone any with clout in the music business."

"No, man, you don't get in the club without someone openin' the door for ya. You gotta know somebody. All I need's a break. It'd be no sweat off your back."

"I'd really love to help you, Sal, but I just stumbled into getting my book published, and it hasn't made such a big hit that *I'm* anybody that people would come to for advice on music."

"So how'd you get published?"

Nathaniel leaned toward Sal like he was going to tell him a secret, "The lady, Sybil, she snuck back to the house and took the manuscript. All I did was sign a form and cash the check."

Sal leaned back in his chair, giving the impression, though with no particular gesture or facial expression, that he was disappointed and a little bit skeptical. "So you were just lucky is what you're sayin'."

"Exactly. I don't know why she did it, but that was my in."

Sal seemed to mull this over for a second, then asked, "Where's she?"

"Your guess is as good as mine. I guess you could find her at the publisher's office in New York. Other than that, I haven't a clue." Then he added, "I haven't spoken to her since we all left the Pequod."

Just then, with a woman's perfect timing, Jen returned to the table. "Is he boring you with his literary talk?" she asked Sal.

Nathaniel stood, Sal following his lead, and motioned toward the horn player. "Jen, this is Sal; Sal, this is my fiancé, Jen."

"Very nice to meet you," Jen spoke first. "You were really great up there."

Sal smiled, if only slightly, and said, "Thanks. It's too bad more people don't get to hear me."

Nathaniel wished that he could see through Sal's dark glasses. He didn't like the idea that Sal might think that he was lying about not being able to help him with his career. He considered whether he might not be able to help Sal after all if they went to New York together. But Jen saved him from making a suggestion that he knew he would regret before he had decided to make it by announcing that she was very tired and wanted to go home.

She smiled at Sal, and they all said goodnight. As Nathaniel walked out the door with Jen holding his arm, he was still bothered by the idea that Sal might think that he was lying, and he wished that there were something that he could do.

The house lights come on to drive away the few remaining stragglers, driving away only the darkness and with it the mystical atmosphere. The room is dingy and sticky. On the floor, the dust clings to spilled drinks like so many tiny, fiendish drunks. One of the waiters appears from the back with a mop, followed by another with a rag and a bottle of blue liquid. They hurry through the motions of cleaning so that they can leave, either to go home or to find some other bar that hasn't dispersed its magic quite so early.

As if the disintegrated dream and the odor of cleanser is enough to accomplish what the light could not, even the most reluctant patrons make their way sullenly through the door into the cool night. Then the staff, some tired, but most impatient to be elsewhere, begins to leave to the sounds of cash drawers slamming shut and chairs being thrown atop tables.

Soon the owner emerges from a door marked "Employees Only" carrying a locked metal box and checks the registers to make sure that they are closed. He gives a quick inspection to the large room that is now as clean as it ever gets. Together with the bouncer, he steps from his place of business into a city that is as quiet as it ever is, not even hearing the rush of cars on adjacent streets or the occasional honking horn or the rumble of a distant train. He locks the door behind them, shakes the knob firmly, and walks, a barely perceptible nervousness in his stride, to his car.

Nathaniel looked out over the ocean, which had not yet turned the reflective, alluring midnight blue of painful waters. The rise and fall of the surface seemed mild and lulling, and he knew that it was still warm. He could, if he wanted, jump in for a swim. He looked down the side of the barnacled wooden boat at the lapping undulations that swept from the bow to the stern and then curled around themselves in swirling, playful hugs before slipping into the rhythm of the rest of the ocean. He felt, through his feet, the rocking of the boat as it drifted along at the slight urging of the tide.

In the distance, he heard the subtle ringing of that seemingly ubiquitous buoy that had come so much to bespeak the coastal ocean that its absence would change entirely the ambiance that nature had done so much to create on its own. It occurred to Nathaniel that the bell might be the perfect emblem of perspective's power: it was simultaneously the herald of a homecoming to society for the seafarer and an omen of endless solitude and inevitability to the landlubber. Nathaniel wondered, though, if it wouldn't take an awfully long journey at sea to reverse the import of the bell when first one has left the land, for the bell had become so much associated with solitude, for Nathaniel, at least, that even the similar timbre of metal rope-weights clanging against an inland flagpole in the night was apt to feel just as lonely, especially when the wind whipped through the flag as through a sail and even more so when an orphaned seagull cawed out miles from the shore.

Here, though, the subtle image was difficult to sustain, because the seagulls kept up such a racket that feelings of solitude were quickly dispersed. Normally, the seagulls' chatter was imperceptibly interwoven with the scenery, but the smell of fish that no amount of bleach or harsh scrubbing could dispel from the boat attracted entire communities of the birds, which hovered in the air, occasionally dipping down to look for the carrion that they felt to be there. One gull was paying particular attention to a pile of knotted netting but darted into the air with a shout when Nathaniel swayed across the deck. He reached between the cords of fraying rope and pealed loose a dry and tacky fluke. It made Nathaniel's stomach churn even to just hold it loosely at arms length by the fin of its tail. He hurled it away. It fell to the water with a sickening slap, and the gulls swarmed down upon it, each trying to rip it from the beak of another until the fish had been torn in half, and they all chased after the two birds that tried to sneak away with their prizes. They nipped at each other and beat their wings against the backs of their neighbors as they grappled for their own little piece of the rotting meat. The wily ones hovered at the edge of the riot and swooped down to gather what little bits of flesh and guts were flung from the carnage. Finally, the twin halves of the fish fell into the water and sank, bits of meat and skin trailing behind them. Some of the gulls dove into the water to salvage what scraps still clung to the bones. Perhaps one or two birds chased it to the bottom. Then the flock floated above the waves and cast one sidelong eye each on Nathaniel as if hoping that he might fling himself overboard.

Glad I'm as big as I am, Nathaniel mused, trying to bring to mind the imperfect comparison that he had heard on the docks...

"Rats of the sea!" yelled a voice from the cabin. Nathaniel had heard the clomping of knee-high rubber boots climbing the stairs from the hold below, where drinks were stowed in piles of ice, and now the wearer of those boots stepped, squinting, into the genial early-Autumn sunlight. He had found a whiting that the lumper had missed among all the ice. The fish gave a weary contraction, and Steinbeck threw it overboard, the seagulls clawing at each other for skimpy bites of the bony fish's body. "Tell me again why you didn't want to take out my sailboat?"

Nathaniel smiled. "I wouldn't want to ruin the polish with my callused feet."

"I don't think she'd mind," Steinbeck told him, meaning the boat. "These rubber boots don't make my feet none too delicate."

Steinbeck handed Nathaniel a soda and opened his beer. It fizzed over as if agitated by the rocking of the boat. They both leaned back on the wooden sideboards, the seagulls sizing them up from behind. Nathaniel commented, "It's always felt kind of fake and arrogant to me to go out on the water in a boat that was only built for pleasure."

"I think you'd change your mind about that if you came out in this utilitarian bucket with me for weeks at a time. It's nice to know the difference between work and play."

"I guess."

"Guess nothin'. You know it so well that you stick with a job that you hate just so's you don't start thinking of it as play, and you've tried so hard to keep your hobbies private for fear that they'd come to feel like work."

"That's not entirely true."

"Well mostly, anyway," Steinbeck took a swig of his beer. "Why do you still bust your ass out here with us workin' men? 'Specially since you've got a chance to make a real career for yourself out of your writing?"

"I like all you workin' men."

"And we like you, but I bet there isn't a man on those docks that wouldn't rather hear about you doin' great things far away than watch you work your way up to foreman hereabouts." He rethought his statement, then, "In a good way."

"I know what you meant, but there's no need to lecture me about it. I've been giving my whole situation some thought."

"That's great. What're you gonna do?"

"Well, I've been thinking about what Sal said..."

"Oh this again!" exclaimed Steinbeck with a chuckle. "You know there's nothing you can do for him right now, and he ought to've known it before he came lookin'."

After sipping his soda, Nathaniel responded, "Well I can understand why he did. I tried for many years, and with different strategies, to get some kind of a break that would help me get to where I could live off of things that I do anyway because I love them, and it wasn't until after I gave up that some strange combination of circumstances and luck gave me a start entirely by accident. It just seems an awfully slim chance on which to hang much hope."

"First of all," Steinbeck began, "it doesn't take but a thread of chance to catch some hope. And second of all, if it was easier it wouldn't mean as much."

"But what a waste to have it mean so much for most people that they never get it. Especially now that everything's marketing and business."

"Well what're you gonna do? There are other ways to be happy. Look at me: I never intended to be a fisherman, but I'm happy with my life, and sometimes I have moments that I wouldn't trade for anything."

"Yeah, but wouldn't you have liked to have a chance?"

"At what?"

Nathaniel was bewildered by this question, though it was one that he had, of course, heard many times before, because it was so foreign to his way of thinking that he hadn't even considered it for his own life.

"Wasn't there ever anything that you wanted to do out of passion for it?" he asked.

Steinbeck's face gave the impression that he was cycling through his memory. "No." he said plainly. "Never anything like you and writing. I mean, I always wanted to be happy, of course, but I just figured I'd set out and hope that eventually the happy moments would maybe equal the not so happy ones. Lately I'm happy just being satisfied."

"Oh how I envy you."

Laughing, Steinbeck countered, "Envy me? What's to envy? I'm happy, sure, but you've got a shot at the big reward."

"And what's that?"

"You might just change the world. You may be miserable most of the time you're doin' it, and you may get to thinking that you're getting nowhere, but at the end of the day I think you'll know that you counted for something. You better, at any rate, otherwise I'll take you out here in old lady *Steadfast* here," Steinbeck gave a good natured slap to the side of the fishing boat and changed tone, feeling as if he ought to lighten the conversation, "and throw you over the side."

Nathaniel turned around and leaned with his forearms against the wooden railing. "I guess you're getting at the way I've been heading with my thoughts. Since I gave up trying to be famous, every day I understand a little bit less why I ever wanted it."

"Well I don't mean to hurry you, but I get the feeling from the buzz I've been hearin' that you're gonna have to make the call soon. What's your plan?"

"I don't know," Nathaniel confessed. "I thought, well I've been thinking more and more, about maybe forming some kind of group to help all the Sals of the world get their shot. Just take all the business out of the whole thing and make it mean something again. I mean, give artists the means and a reason to get better rather than closer to some marketable idea of artistry, whatever that means."

Steinbeck's lips and eyebrows arched in a sign of pensive approval, and he told Nathaniel that he thought it was a great idea, sincerely. "Be tough, though," he appended.

Smiling with sweet cynicism, Nathaniel replied, "Well it wouldn't mean as much if it was easy."

15

They were both quiet for a moment. They were treading waters that were far too deep for such a pleasant and still afternoon, and neither was still young and innocent enough to imagine that their Sunday talk might instantly solve the world's problems. Better, perhaps, to leave Sundays to drifting fancies and conversations of gentle rocking. Steinbeck wanted to ask one more question before they sank into the repose that they both knew was imminent. "What're you gonna call it?"

Looking sidelong at Steinbeck while putting the soda can to his lips, Nathaniel let out an amused thrill of air through his nose. "I was thinking maybe *Timshel.*"

Steinbeck let out a hearty laugh and slapped Nathaniel on the back. "Sounds like a good name to me!" he said.

A good, hopeful name indeed! Even the seagulls seem to flutter about with slightly more anticipation. Their anticipation, however, may owe more to the fact that the men on the good ship Steadfast *have stirred, one going below deck, and they think by their sense of smell from far above in the air that the innards of the boat store fish enough for all to get their fill. But, being birds, they do not understand that the boat has been emptied for the insatiable humans, and all that is stored under the boards is ice and intoxicating fluid. Perhaps, if the man who took all the fish from the hold to earn his own singular living had overlooked some morsel in his haste to fill his baskets, then there will be some small treat for them when the captain returns aboveboard. But they will have to claw each other's backs and snap at each other's beaks to get even just a taste, more often the taste of blood than that of fish, though whether they are still capable of the distinction is a matter of some doubt.*

No, hope is an abstraction, no matter how we might feel it to have substance. It cannot be woven into platters, though, in a sense, it may be shattered. Hope flutters, perhaps glisteningly, for a moment, but the object to which it is tied slaps against unpredictable reality and is quickly consumed, and what is not claimed cannot do otherwise than sink below our reach until another chance is fabricated out of the misty air.

As the sun peeked slyly over the ocean at the fleeing moon, the machine whirred. Its metal slats scraped an occasional rasp against the walls along the sides of the mesh belt as they were dragged up and over and under and back into the salt water. The water frothed along the edges of the stainless steel tub and spun irritable ripples along the surface; underneath, it was roiled by the belt and twirled in a current as it was sucked through a tube and spit out onto the wooden planks. Rubber boots slopped across the slimy boards followed by the metal wheels of mechanized yellow palette-jacks piled high with empty waxed cardboard boxes that were being tossed in rows along the sides of the dock. Gnarled loops of thick rope thudded against the lids of the boxes and set them rocking as the cords slid down posts and tightened into splintered grooves. The sides of the boat thumped against the worn wood and made the whole dock shudder. A cloud of smoke billowed out invisibly against the dark gray sky as the boat's engine gave a final thrust against the tide and was cut off. Huge, white, and stained buckets swung over the boat on ropes and floated into the hole in the deck, disappearing into the hold. They tottered as they reappeared, spilling whiting onto the deck, into the water, and onto the dock. The fish were dumped into a chute and rolled through the lime-colored plastic tubes in waves of cool salt water. The whiting churned over and around each other as the chute dipped and curved and emptied them out into the tub of the steel machine, where they seethed with the water and were caught by the metal slats, which carried them over the mesh metal belt and dumped those that it did not shred onto the scale-encrusted cull-board. Bodies with torn and spilling guts were plucked from the surge of fish and tossed into the grimy water of the harbor, where the seagulls finished the disembowelment that the machine had begun. The whole fish were pushed along by a rubber glove and fell into a chain-linked basket on a rusting scale. In response to an uttered "yawp," the glove held up the flow of whiting while Nathaniel lifted the sixty-pound basket and poured its contents into a cardboard box, and the box was whisked away.

The men chattered as they worked, spilling rude jokes and spitting barely sensical exclamations into the air. They shouted to each other about drinking and gambling and women. They tossed good-spirited insults to their friends and roared baldfaced lies of rumors along the line.

Nobody believed any of it. The red-eyed box-maker shouted a boorish question to the lanky palette-wrapper, who sneered it at the jack-ass, middle-aged and muscular, who laughed it in a husky voice to the chunky, charismatic foreman. The foreman whispered it to the assistant foreman, who loitered like a shifty toady by his side, and the assistant foreman shouted it like a dirty joke to the boxing team, who passed it around among themselves — from the stocky palette-loader to Nathaniel, the dumper, to the dark and jovial cull-board man, who was missing a finger on his left hand — and then cheered it down the dock in unison to the old, gnarled winch-man. The winch-man cackled it to the bucket-catcher. The bucket-catcher pushed it to the fishermen on the deck of the boat along with an empty bucket, and it followed the bucket through the hole to the lumper in the hold, coming back with a snide answer that followed the fish, the product, back down the line, anticipated with and pursued by roguish mirth.

Meanwhile, another boat docked on the opposite side of the pier, and banter shot back and forth across the boards like cannonballs. The sun was well into morning when the first boat was unloaded, and the second cut loose and lurched across the water to take its place. The dock workers took quick breaks, some staying behind to take a less onerous position on the line, though rank or brawn was likely to supersede the move, and some returning with the faint smell of brandy lingering in the air around their heads.

The second boat was all fluke, flounder, monk, and dogfish. Less weight but more work. Huge green vats were dragged out onto the dock for the monk and dogs. The sun beat down upon Nathaniel, and he began to sweat as he lifted boxes of flatfish onto the palettes in layers of six, five high, eighteen hundred pounds of fish on each before the jack-ass took it away with his yellow machine and Nathaniel slammed another wooden palette against the boards.

Next came lunch. The tourists, a thinning crowd as Autumn overtook New England, passed more hastily now than they had just moments before, when they had slowed to watch the workers as if it weren't work at all, but a reenactment in an authentic outdoor museum and the workers only actors who mimicked the motions of ancient dock-hands in the actual costumes of ages past just as others, elsewhere, took the roles of blacksmiths and candle-makers. Now the workers dropped their rubber overalls around their ankles and sat at a desiccated picnic table to eat and ogle the wives and daughters of passing men, who diverted their eyes and hustled their families along toward the ferry.

After lunch, the workers made their way reluctantly back to the dock, some by way of the bathroom, two by way of the ice room (again, lending a subtle spice to the air when they emerged), to find a boat waiting to unload lobsters and stone crabs. A cloud was spreading across the sky, and the wind picked up, putting a chill in the air.

Now that they had eaten and relaxed, and because lobsters and crabs are packed more lightly and make for slower, more careful work, the wind seemed to freeze their sweat- and sea-soaked shirts against their skin, and one by one they slipped away to add layers of clothing. They knew, though, that they would strip it all again when they got into the groove of unloading the next boat, a big one that was already strapped to the posts.

It was mid-afternoon by the time Nathaniel paused to take off his heavy flannel shirt, and he had just slipped his hands into his grimy rubber gloves when the foreman stuck his head out of the office window and shouted that Nathaniel had a visitor.

Someone said, loud enough for all to hear, "See that? Once yer famous y'ain't no good for workin'; can't put t'gether a whole day 'n less'n a week."

Everybody laughed, including Nathaniel, and they all laughed again when the dark-skinned cull-board man with the missing finger yelled out, "Herry up 'n sign yer ahtographs, boy, an' get yer ass back here. Theh's work ta do!"

Nathaniel slipped off his gloves as he stepped inside the barn-like building that housed the office. He could hear the thirty-five inch television on which the foremen and their boss liked to watch basketball games. He walked toward the sound but stopped when a familiar voice called out his name from behind him.

He turned and said, "Holden! What are you doing here?"

Holden shuffled his feet on the new wood floor, still covered with sawdust, as if he had more of a confession than a request to make. Then he swung right into his pitch, "Listen Nathaniel. I've come a long way to do you a favor, and I'm not gonna insult you by beating around the bush."

"Well it's mighty fine to see you, too," Nathaniel said, smiling because he wanted it to be an ambiguous joke.

"My father runs *Ethos* magazine. Have you heard of it?"

"Yeah, who hasn..."

"Well your book's really taking off with our readers, and it would really be a great promotional tool for you to let me write an interview with you."

"What... wait... I, I haven't been looking to do any promotional interviews."

"Exactly!" Holden exclaimed as if his point had been made and the matter settled. "That's why nobody has printed it yet. And I wanna be the first."

Nathaniel shoved his gloves in the pockets of the jeans that he wore under his rubber overalls and looked at Holden with bewildered eyes that hinted, though only slightly, that he foresaw impending helplessness. "Despite the fact that you've appeared from nowhere and sprung this on me without showing the slightest interest in visiting with me, Holden, I appreciate what you want to do for me, but it's a path that I don't want to start walking. I want to let the book do what it has in it to do on its own, but without involving me."

Appearing to rear up a bit, Holden took the tone of an elder brother, "Nathaniel, I know you think of me as a kid, but I've seen enough to know that one of two things will happen: either the book will lose steam without promotional pushes from you, or it'll take off anyway and drag you along." Then, poking his left hand with his right pointer finger, "You have to get control now or you'll lose it altogether, and if you start it off with a friend, you can be sure to start it off in a good way."

"No."

Holden threw his hands in the air, "Why are you being so stubborn?"

"I'm not being stubborn," Nathaniel replied, keeping his composure though he was slightly displaced from reality by the rapid pace at which Holden moved in his thoughts, changing, entirely, the mood of the day for Nathaniel in mere seconds, "I've given this a lot of thought and have made up my mind to stay out of it. Even the fact that it was published had nothing to do with me."

Holden laughed sardonically, "Nothing to do with you?" He laughed. "You wrote the goddam thing!"

Nathaniel shook his head with an expression that confirmed his words, "Believe what you want, but I'm not going to change my mind. I'm sorry you came all this way just to find it out."

With his demeanor making the transition from advisor to helpless friend to fretting child, Holden first shook his head, then, turning his back on Nathaniel, stomped his foot, finally flailing his arms from over his head to his sides, where they slapped his thighs. Nathaniel watched the transformation patiently.

With his temper petering out as if being flung off in pieces with each wave of an arm, Holden turned to face Nathaniel. "Well if you won't do it for your stupid self, why don't you do it for me?"

"What difference does it make to you?"

Holden bowed his head, preparing to make a confession, "Listen... I'm the owner's son, and I haven't really had a big story or idea yet, so nobody really takes me seriously. And I... I'm just sick of feeling like everybody is talking behind my back and thinking that I'm getting an easy ride. I mean, I may not be a bigshot reporter or nothing, with all the stars ringing my phone off the hook or great as hell stories falling into my lap, but I do work."

Nathaniel was reticent to offer too much consolation but tried to present a noncommittal comfort by saying, "Holden, I'm sure you'll find something big if you keep at it long enough."

"But you could be it." His confidence was rebuilding. "I mean, if you gave me an interview, I'm sure other things would follow. All it takes is one break. You know that."

"No, I disagree. It takes a long time and hard work."

Holden's confidence slipped and his temper splashed up, "Oh whatta you know? Everything's come to you on a platter. You don't even want to do the work of an interview."

"It's not that."

"It *is* that! All you do is throw your fish around all winter and then sit in the woods picking your nose all summer, then somebody publishes a

book you wrote and people are talking about you like you're the next...
the next J.D. goddam Salinger, and you won't even help out a friend.
Who wants a friend like that? I'd help you out if I was this big famous
author and all."

"Holden, I'm sorry, I just don't want to..."

"To go down that path, I know. You said that already. Can't you think
of something new to say for Chrissakes? It's a miracle you finished a
book at all!" Holden stomped his foot and put his hands on his hips,
saying, "Well, I didn't want to have to do it, but if you're not going to
help me out, I don't have a choice."

As if his ears had perked up, Nathaniel's eyes flashed, and in a harsh
tone he asked, knowing that his was precisely the expected reaction,
"What do you mean?"

"Oh you know what I mean. I saw the way you used to act, and you
can't tell me that there isn't a world of dirt out there on you. That'd be
an even *bigger* story, and you know it. I wasn't going to do it because I
thought you were my friend and all, even though I knew it would be a
better story."

"You wouldn't know how to begin looking," Nathaniel said, getting
angry.

"Oh I've read your notebooks. I know where to start, and you can't
stop me."

"You better bet I can stop you! If you so much as..."

The foreman stepped out of the office looking large and imposing in
the dark corridor, "Hey Nate, is this guy giving you a problem?"

Holden raised his hands in a defensive, dismissive gesture and said,
"No. No problem. I was just leaving. I have to catch a train to New
Jersey. Nathaniel, I'll see you later."

With that, as quickly as he had appeared with his tornado plea,
Holden slipped out the door and was gone. Nathaniel was about to
chase after him but paused as the foreman spoke. "Is everything
alright?"

Going slack, Nathaniel responded in a distant voice, "Yeah, he can go
to New Jersey, but I don't think he'll know what to do once he's there."

A car horn tooted, and Nathaniel heard the sound of tires trying to
peel out on gravel. "Yeah," he said, "he's nothing to worry about."

The foreman slapped him on the back and said, "Whatever you say, Nate, but let me know if I can do anything for you."

Nathaniel stands looking out the doorway as the foreman walks back to the office and to the television. The sound of disparate drops of rain begins to reverberate through the empty wooden room. Going out into the fresh air, Nathaniel crosses to the storage room and emerges wearing a plastic raincoat. He looks at the sky as if refreshed by the slight drops that fall onto his face and slide down his neck.

He walks out onto the dock, the other workers brushing by him as they use the rain as an excuse for a break, if only one long enough to put on rain gear. With the dock momentarily cleared, Nathaniel is free to choose a station, and instead of trying to get away with taking one of the easier ones, he stands ready in a position that nobody will begrudge him. Ready to dump baskets.

A Whispering Through the Branches
by Justin Katz
(Timshel Literature, 2001)

Available on the island at:
    Island Books, 575 East Main Road, Middletown
    Thames Street Books, 433 Thames St., Newport

Or online at www.timshelarts.com

Or call (401) 835-7156 for more information

Born on the Cadence

Ingrid Mathews

Born on the cadence
Of the ever changing tide
Dawn's reflective light
Fleetingly caresses
The shifting sands of time
Painting the shoreline
With its myriad colors
Acquiescing to the changing light

Ingrid Mathews

Are Adults Too Old for Young Adult Literature?

Len DeAngelis

N̄o.

When asked how much time they spend reading, most adults would say, "Not enough." A suggestion about a reading area to compete with other reading obligations and choices deserves an argument. Time is limited. If readers inject something new, something old has to go, or the time for it abbreviated to accommodate. However, employing the NIKE advice, "Just do it," challenges. Considering *why* one should precedes *how* one should — the latter being too personal to tackle collectively, and each of us makes time for what we want to do.

Adults reflecting on their growth usually point to the teen years as jarring, and guiding and watching others experience this stage evokes memories, conversation, and reflection. I have devoted my life to teens because they exemplify opposites: good, bad, exciting, dull, boring, interesting, tolerant, intolerant, listening, deaf, respectful, disrespectful — the list is endless. Often they don't seek guidance and advice because they want to find out for themselves. Most adults try to make those discoveries as painless as possible, and some make teen life more complicated and painful. Those of us who have stuck with teens in spite of many turn-offs know they need interested adults. They may persist in camouflaging themselves and drive full-speed toward exasperation, but we stay for the ride, checking our seat belts and airbags and offering prayers.

My preference as a writer is teens. I have centered my life's work around them, and, when staring at a blank page, I usually decide to write for them and about them because they read and listen. Many won't give the satisfaction of comprehension at a moment of disagreement, but let time pass, and if an adult hangs around long enough, and if the moment is resurrected, an appreciation may come forth. It may not.

The appreciation doesn't matter as much to me as the drive to offer teens the lifelines of experience. As an audience, that age group allows me to dabble into preteen and childhood experiences, as well as those well beyond, in an effort to forecast possibilities. The wisdom of the aged, carefully presented, strikes a hit. And if it doesn't, the exercise is worth the effort just because it makes good sense, and teens wouldn't have it if it weren't offered. Sure, they can lump and dump, but, more often than not, they savor and record.

Teens have an energy and excitement about life. The breadth of possibilities from the gamut of life's span invites creativity — the spark of life. That satisfies me.

Writing for them means reading about them. From that reading, adults can learn lessons that are worth the time adjustment. Often, adults only have time for reviews, such as the collection that follows.

A Year Down Yonder, by Richard Peck (Dial Books for Young Readers, 2000)

A survey conducted by *Parade,* a weekend-newspaper insert, investigated movie stars' wishes for the new year. Gwyneth Paltrow wished for a book that she could not put down. My suggestion: *A Year Down Yonder,* by Richard Peck. An author who sets the standard for middle-school–age students, Richard Peck has created a lovely story in this Newbery Medal book that flows like sweet cream to its "happily every after" ending.

The recession of 1937 caused more ripples in families than did any of the recent economic periods to which the label has been applied. In its midst, Mary Alice goes to live with her grandmother in an Illinois hick town. Grandmother is formidable, and boy readers will appreciate the cleverness with which she takes on challenges and maintains her reputation.

A city girl, Mary Alice faces grandmother, school, and her own growth over the course of the year depicted in the book. Mary Alice's classmates and her ingenuity (perhaps a chip off grandmother's block, no doubt gene-descendent) create a warmth that invigorates. The humor is feisty, and the depiction of this slice of Americana is presented with originality. Mr. Peck injects cleverly worded phrases, some that sound like clichés, in a context that is fresh and consistent with the observations of a fifteen year old.

A Year Down Yonder is a sequel to *A Long Way from Chicago,* and fans will ask when they may expect *its* sequel. And to Gwyneth: This is not a book to be read between scenes, or the director will be stopping the cameras until the preoccupied reader detaches herself from the book.

Stargirl, by Jerry Spinelli (Knopf, 2000)

When I first heard the title of Jerry Spinelli's book, *Stargirl,* I thought of a girl who stood out in my thirty-two years in the classroom. She was small, winsome, and quiet, with pixie-ish hair, and she wore lots of black clothes and, sometimes, almond-shaped glasses that tapered. She didn't act out as Stargirl does, but the more I read, the closer Mr. Spinelli came to depicting the character of my student, who many didn't see or take the time to appreciate. Her individuality was a trademark that she exhibited but did not impose and rarely shared except in her writing. The book cover, very cleverly simple, tactile, symbolic, and aptly colored, displays a five-pointed star and a bald stick figure in a triangle-dress.

In the book, Leo Borlock tells the story of his ninth-grade year at age fourteen, when Stargirl Caraway, birth-named Susan Julia Caraway, appeared for her junior year. Home-schooled, Stargirl is a free spirit. Leo, in his overly mature manner describes her on page 107 as, "bendable light: she shone around every corner of my day." The book is peppered with these expressions that are beyond the level of a ninth grader but act as clues to identify the narrator. The first is on page 27: "The atmosphere bristled like cactus paddles."

Most teens pride themselves on their individuality but are reluctant to express it. They like being accepted by others more than they like developing themselves — not Stargirl. Leo and Stargirl connect, and he experiences the exhilaration of her individuality and develops a crush that sears his heart until he gets shunned. Then Leo feels invisible, and even Stargirl attempts to be accepted. The adult voice in the book is presented through Archibald Hapwood Brubaker, a paleontologist with a gift, who recognizes and appreciates Stargirl's individuality.

Stargirl vanishes as she appeared, leaving the reader wondering if she was an apparition whose impact is life long. Her story makes the message of her being and values emphatic. There are people and characters we never forget; Stargirl is one such individual. Spinelli creates a story that resonates, breeds discussion and analysis, and can stand on its own as a good read once or time and time again.

You Don't Know Me, David Klass (Farrar, Straus & Giroux, 2001)

A man sat on a park bench muttering audibly, a book in hand, with a professorial demeanor. In balmy weather more indicative of summer than of November 20, passers-by walked, ran, ate, and chatted during lunch-time at Baltimore's Inner Harbor. I slowed my pace on my first pass, attracted to the man repeating "know." Painters paint publicly. Why couldn't readers read publicly? Perhaps he tried to block out the interference to his concentration. He didn't look to be reading-challenged.

On my return pass, I observed the scene and stood comfortably apart from him, but within listening distance. He was still on page one. I left. At 3:00 p.m., he was introduced to ALAN (The Assembly on Literature for Adolescents) Workshop participants as David Klass, and I worried that my eavesdropping might be labeled "author stalking," even if I had not connected the man and his craft. Then, when he read a familiar sentence, I questioned whether I mightn't be labeled worse than that — same verb, different tense, same object. "Hey," I wanted to shout, "After more revisions than I cared to track, my book's first sentence is dangerously close to yours!" I kept the thought to myself, satisfied that differences and similarities occur and that I had miles to go before publication.

After he read the first page, I thought about the reading order that I had considered for the books provided by ALAN (compliments of generous publishers) and saved *You Don't Know Me* as a revision-reward read. When I finally opened it, I ate the pages, allowing food temptations to stale.

Riveting. Compelling. I broke up the reading to savor the impact.

John's father left him and his mom. When John sees a thread of satisfaction for his mother with her live-in boyfriend, he keeps the man's abuse to himself. The man intimidates and threatens John, but John's surging manhood, making him feel responsible for returning his mother's sacrifices, silences him.

John's narration of his ninth-grade life includes a cast of characters named to suit his feelings for them. Ms. Moonface, his math teacher, when called that directly, reacts to name calling with the hurt and injury any kid camouflages better but feels as piercingly. John is no angel but is an individual, and Mr. Steinwilly's persistence and sensitivity works.

Glory Hallelujah is John's fantasy girl. A date scene made me wonder, with all of the warning (and the libido raging) there, how John ends the night, which borders on being contrived and far-fetched, nearly skinned. The night's continuation into frigid torment plunges the reader into a vortex that rattles, even vicariously.

At times, the narrator's story does read like a verbal exercise — for example, "flocculent snow" on page 240. But, there are sentences to savor, though they are profound for a ninth grader, such as this on p.147: "Allow me to share one simple and very frightening truth with you: your real enemy is someone who knows you. And the better they know you, and the closer they are to you, the greater is their capacity to do you harm." Great, but better for an adult to express, like Mr. Hayes's statement on p. 229: "It doesn't matter how you look, or how people look at you — what's important is how you look at yourself." A truism that bears repeating in a variety of expressions.

The violence at the end of the book rivals any by Stephen King but underscores what it takes to get people to hear as well as listen. Although there is some difficulty around the boy's imaginings, the well-paced plot proceeds, and the subplots offset the focus on the abuse theme, placing it as a carat among baguettes. John's tensions, apprehensions, and fears connect us to a young life, experiencing what has the potential to become damaging memories. Through this young adult, adults can learn about perpetuating and breaking cycles.

Jerome, by William Taylor (Alyson Publications, 1999)

The reader learns about Jerome Winter through chats, faxes, and emails from two friends whom he left behind when he died: Marco Petrovic in New Zealand and Katie in the U.S.A. The threesome met each other in Atherton, New Zealand. Soon after Katie leaves as a foreign exchange student, Marco writes to her of Jerome's demise.

Through their writings, family issues and tensions spice up the dialogue but never compete with the focus of their relationship: learning about each other and helping each other survive this fact of life. Most of the idioms are understandable contextually, though "had his guts for garters" may demand translation into each language in which the book is printed.

Katie and Marco write in young adult language that may cause adults to limit the book's availability – Taylor makes "fuck" the thirteenth word of the opening chapter. But protest will certainly increase the readership because kids want to read what they are forbidden. This book, however, deserves their attention for other reasons, mostly because it reflects characters experiencing growth. Though thoroughly red-neck in attitude, Marco shatters like a door of glass hit by a boulder when Katie returns to New Zealand for a holiday break in December. The three friends are reunited at Jerome's grave in a climax and ending that pull the reader into a vortex in 95 pages.

Because of the book's brevity, questions and thoughts will simmer and make readers eager to talk about issues like values, stereotypes, prejudice, suicide, rape, family relationships, smoking, booze, bullying, cultures, friendships, and the tangents each of these stimulate. Who is the magnetic-filings-image on the cover?

The author does a masterful job of listening and imparting a fraction of narration, allowing the kids to expose the story. Katie and Marco may not be quoted in years to come, but they will be remembered for writing and speaking a profound story.

A Cold Case, Philip Gourevitch (Farrar, Straus & Giroux, 2001)

Although this is an adult book, my class read an article by the author that allowed them to view a video tape of Koehler's confession, via a guest lecturer. Teens are interested in adult issues. Philip Gourevitch's *A Cold Case* is a "cold" story — one that has already been "told," nearly in its entirety, in issues of *The New Yorker*. In the book, there's a bit more background on the tenacious investigator, Andy Rosenzwieg, who gets his man, Frankie Koehler, with Frankie's cooperation, after twenty-seven years.

The book's 184 pages can be read as quickly as the magazine that forecasted and was the setting for the story. What makes the book worth the additional investment — beyond the magazine subscription — are two minor figures, insight into Koehler's mind and his advice, and good writing.

Gourevitch writes in a style as smooth as soft ice cream, yet facts amass. He manages to insert tidbits of information that elaborate on what is known about the case, but the book is not a mystery because an aware reader knows the ending. What intrigues the reader is how the story came together — its history.

A Cold Case presents a Koehler, other than the criminal, who begs for more development: Koehler's wife is an interesting woman who deserves more attention. A picture of old-school love and loyalty, she provides a rationale for why Koehler became the person that he became: rejection. Therein is one lesson. The other stunning lesson of the book comes from Karen McGinn-Hagen, who was six when her thirty-eight year old father, Peter, was shot by Koehler. What her father and his children (four of them) missed out on, what Koehler "blew away," is expressed in her evocative testimony.

Gourevitch serves his readers well. He could have served them better by adding written pictures of the victims beyond those at the murder scene and of family members (if they allowed). Further statements from participants and perhaps articles from newspapers covering the case would have provided a broader comprehension than the book enables. A transcript of the confession videotape, which I have seen and heard parts of on NPR, should not await the movie. But readers' wanting more is a rewarding testament to a writer's investment of time and talent.

A *Cup of Tea,* by Amy Ephron (Ballantine, 1998)

Amy Ephron's *A Cup of Tea* is a predictable beach read with less density and depth than the liquid and its holder in the title. Set in 1917 New York, the noire element established by the author reaches an unsurprising exposure in a dramatic ending that imitates O'Henry poorly because it lacks cleverness.

The pattern is familiar: debutante helps Cinderella, mix in the debutante's prince's testosterone, army hitch, army error, a girlfriend, and, voila, there are Rosemary, Philip, and Jane racing through fast-paced chapters that lack substance. The characters have a semblance of believability, but they are sacrificed to the plot instead of the reverse.

Plainsong, by Kent Haruf (Vintage Contemporaries, 2000)

Plainsong may leave your hands, but not your head, and if you let it, it will touch your heart. Kent Haruf tells a third-person story by changing the characters who serve as subjects for each chapter, an alteration of the technique used by Chaucer and contemporary writers Barbara Kingsolver (*The Poisonwood Bible*) and Andre Dubus III (*House of Sand and Fog*), who all change narrators through a work.

Disregarding quotation marks, as Frank McCourt does in *Angela's Ashes,* Haruf dabbles into his characters — as an artist selects paints from a palette — until the last three pages, when the palette itself vacuums the story and reader into a vortex. With casual but careful perception, Haruf's strokes splay into the essence of his plot, unfolding the chapters in a manner that entices the reader with each sentence and paragraph. The title, as defined on an opening page, means "the unisonous vocal music used by the Christian church from the earliest times; any simple or unadorned melody or air." However, the significance of the title is best understood by reading the book.

Tom Guthrie, a teacher/single parent; Victoria Roubideaux, a pregnant teenager; Ike and Bobby (Guthrie), 10 and 9, respectively; McPherons (Harold and Raymond), crude men hurt by gossip; Ella (Guthrie), a woman in search of herself; and Maggie Jones, a teacher/daughter, are the characters who serve as chapter subjects. Through them, Haruf presents a town with a cast of minor characters, including Judy, the school secretary; Lloyd Crowder, the school principal, a "fat tub of guts" in Mr. Beckman's (a parent) words; and Iva Stearns, whose smoke and clutter permeate the page. Each character is a masterpiece of sensitivity and detail, and, seen in the panoramic display that Haruf creates, each contributes to the author's purpose of presenting a contemporary American town where life happens.

Haruf blends humor and sex into his story. Ike assesses Ralph Black for Bobby as "just an old dogfart." The way in which the McPherons rid themselves of an unwanted visitor is just what the reader roots for them to do. Ike and Bobby watch older kids engaging in sex. (How many young people continue to learn about sex accidentally?) The violence and abuse unfolds in a manner that makes the reader grimace and wish he or she could jump into the page.

Haruf includes a segment on the school issue of parents defending a child. Any student, parent, teacher, or administrator can associate with the characters playing these roles. It is believable. What gratifies about Haruf's work is that he keeps the characters in character. Other aspects lack the clarification to satisfy. Must the reader assume Ike and Bobby are left unsupervised when their father acts "single"? And on page 157, a sentence reads, "Then she [Judy] told him [Tom] the story about the blonde on the charter plane to Hawaii, and in turn he asked if she knew what the worst thing was for someone to say to you when you were standing at the urinal."

What distinguishes Haruf and *Plainsong* is that he strums the reader's emotions and interest — especially as the reader thinks about the story after completing the book. This reader wishes Haruf had left less to my imagination and carried each exposed item to a sensible and definitive "Harufian" resolution. However, reading groups need to speculate, and too neat a package leaves the characters and the story on a shelf instead of in the mind. Overall, *Plainsong* is an engaging piece of writing that resonates in its simplicity.

Haruf has also written *The Tie That Binds* and *Where You Once Belonged*. *Plainsong*, itself, is a *New York Times* Notable Book, a *New Yorker* Book Award Finalist, Winner of the Mountains & Plains Booksellers Association Award, and a National Book Award Finalist. When you buy this book, buy two — one to own and one to loan. As a gift, this book needs no wrapping.

Whale Talk, by Chris Crutcher (Greenwillow, 2001)

Buy this book, but *do not read it* unless you are willing to order in or eat cereal and delay everything else on your schedule.

Judy Crosby, of Island Books, Middletown, RI, and I have a contest going: she stacks copies of Chris Crutcher's *Ironman,* and almost every time I go into the bookstore, I deplete her supply. One of us will tire eventually. I buy the copies to give as gifts for weddings, birthdays, retirements, and any event worth gifting. Yesterday, while checking out with this visit's installment to my library, she said, "Oh, I've been saving something for you. I know you have an order in for April, but here's my copy." *Whale Talk.*

For those of us who are addicted to Chris Crutcher's books, the wait since 1996 left us rereading previous works. Chris canned one book so as "not to be the guy who exploited that tragedy [in Littleton, Colorado] for personal gain." Now, the bookshelf holds a new creation: *Whale Talk,* from Greenwillow Books. The publisher could better serve readers by sprucing up covers. Another detail that this reader would like is for the person to whom Crutcher dedicated the book, Ben Dodge (1982-1997), to be identified. Though not a short story, the 219 page book can be read in one sitting — sorely.

Chris characteristically creates subjects who deserve attention and repair. The narrator of *Whale Talk* is The Tao Jones (The Dow Jones), who possesses an "exotic DNA," is physically fulfilled, and comes from a stable and supportive family unit. He assembles a swim team for Cutter High that resembles pieces of a puzzle stuck together. The crew from Mr. Nakatani's Anger Management Class (see *Ironman*) has been replaced by a cross-section of students who beg for justice and development and extract emotion.

Crutcherese is a dialect of prose imitative of Swift's satire and Gracie Allen's quick wit for taking a cue and turning it inside out to create humor. Two examples: "The swim team from the Sahara" (p. 46) and "Spock, are you out of your Vulcan mind?"(p.12). Language that some will find offensive spices up *Whale Talk* frequently because that's how kids speak.

Georgia Brown is developed like a song, and Abby Jones is the epitome of sense and sensibility, but early on in the book, Crutcher pays unnecessary attention to Mark Furhman and Charleton Heston. How The Tao's adopted parents met deserves development, as does keeping Abby Jones present until the ending. My two favorite teens in this book were Chris Coughlin and Andy Mott, who will hopefully make an appearance again, perhaps in an expansion of *Athletic Shorts.* Andy may be a "less is more" formation, but his experiences deserve to be explored in more depth.

There are gruesome elements to this book that rival King and attest to the range of the truth of fiction. Some readers may close the book and let the violence settle before returning to see how Crutcher has dealt with it for us. But readers need not doubt the conglomeration of facts that Crutcher presents because anyone who knows, or wants to know, the world in which young adults live, will realize that the author's imagination *aligned* incidents, not necessarily creating them from scratch. Life does that for us. People hurt other people.

Through his works, Crutcher speaks for kids and advocates in a manner that should make his books required reading for adults. Kids read him because they trust his truth. *Whale Talk* gives readers one more Crutcher novel to reread until the next book appears, hopefully without postponement in reaction to another tragedy.

Boy Still Missing, by John Searles (William Morrow & Co., 2001)

Boy Still Missing, by John Searles, fulfills the jacket praise of Frank McCourt ("bid your family and friends *au revoir*"), Wally Lamb (who "read — hungrily, compulsively, worried sick for... a character"), and Chris Bohjalian ("moving, intelligent, and gripping debut"). In its 292 pages, ten chapters, plus a prologue and epilogue, Mr. Searles proves his mastery of the technique of making the reader read faster: write an interesting book, with rapid plot changes, unraveling the mystery of the past while complicating the events of the present.

Mr. Searles also wrote an article in *The New York Times* (March 25, 2001) in which Clyde, his stylist, who shares the name of a minor character, led him through a series of publicity photos for his book that focused on the unnecessary glamour in lieu of the Stacy Sheehan photo that captured the core of the man.

"The way the world pinballed me that year [1971-1972]" is how Dominick Prindle, the older narrator, reflects on his life during his fifteenth year. Mr. Searles portrays Dominick accurately: lonely, self-conscious, sexually concentrated, bumbling, loving, considerate, sweet, foolish, thoughtful, and thoughtless. Consequences? Kids forsake them, if they think of them at all, because this is the time of their lives to experiment. They are invulnerable. They want their weak, changing voices heard. When no one gives them the attention they deserve and need, they act — without experience and without wisdom because they lack those characteristics. Teens, if they survive, learn best by their mistakes, as do the adults around them.

Between Holedo, Massachusetts, and New York City, Dominick collides with real world events. Through what he does and what he doesn't do, life happens. The people he encounters demonstrate the range of the truth of fiction. Aspects of the book are far-fetched or coincidental. Humor and symbols are incorporated like spices in this emotional stew of a book that will have the reader racing through paragraphs to see how the author deals with each turn of events that he creates. One races ahead to get the answers, aware of the ability to go back to fill in the details after the "what happens" is known.

Searles gives social issues vent while the violence and media indicative of this age surge. The title of the book, found in Uncle Donald's Bible, is a well-crafted metaphor for Dominick's life.

John Searles has written a novel worth reading.

Granda

Christine L. Mullen

Filtered sunlight and traces of a rainbow visible out the two big front fifth-floor windows looking out over Murdieson Street, a steep street going all the way up to the Whin Hill. Morag's Granny is bending over the black sink washing her face with a square of wool blanket, worn thin, and green Fairy soap. Her steel-gray hair is plaited to her waist. Morag's Granda is sitting with his back to her making "spills" to light his pipe from the edges of The Daily Telegraph. The middle parts are torn into squares for toilet paper, which he'll hang on a nail in the lavatory, shared with the two other tenants on the landing.

Morag sits opposite her Granda waiting for her Granny to undo her plait, to bend over from the waist, throwing her hair down in front to comb it. All the while carrying on a discussion, the content of which Morag has no idea.

"...so a saaz, saaz I aye... ...so she saaz ach yer haverin..."

Her Granny twists her hair into a bun at the nape of her slim, sinewy neck, holds it in place with various bone hairpins, and heads toward the lobby cupboard to pull on her long gray pinstripe wool coat with a separate fox fur collar. She comes back in to see herself in the foggy dresser mirror as she carefully places her black wide-brimmed hat held at just the right angle with a pearl hat pin on her smoothed hair.

"Johnny, hand me that accumulator; may as well get it recharged while I'm in that vicinity. I win't be many meenits tae am back."

"Ach ya auld Hun you know damn well ye're gonna be at The Snug 'ti' we have tae come and get ye."

"Johnny Murphy hold yer tongue... talking like that in front o' that wean."

As her Granda takes a deep breath and gets ready to say more — "hold yer tongue will ye."

"Granda can I have a bit o' cheese?" Morag knows how to get his attention. He sets the spills and squares of newspaper aside, takes the big black kettle from the hob, and puts it on the gas stove to speed the water to a boil for his tea. He holds thick slices of day-old bread to the glowing coals with a long-handled fork until the Willow-pattern bread plate is piled high with golden toasted bread, burned around the edges. Morag waits patiently for him to cut the hard sweaty cheddar into bite-sized cubes because he knows that's the way she likes it and her mother did, too, at her age. He pours his tea into a blue and white bowl with lots of sugar and milk then slurps it, wetting his handlebar moustache. Morag waits for him to pour some into a china saucer — it cools faster — for her to slurp in-between fingers of toast and cheese.

from The Congregation

Lori Dillman

Prelude

In 1720, almost 100 years to the day since the first Pilgrims set foot on Plymouth Rock, a small group of Connecticut settlers met in the home of Nathaniel Haynes to discuss the formation of a local church. The wives could not be spared from the never-ending household chores and the care of the youngest settlers, so the men carried back the word. During the long winter months, weekly Sunday services would be held at various centrally located farms in the community. In the spring and summer, weather permitting, the congregation would meet under the giant oak in Nathaniel's east pasture.

The first service was held in December in Mr. Haynes's front parlor, causing his wife to engage in a flurry of activity beforehand to make sure the room was suitable to receive the Lord, not to mention the wives and families of their fellow farmers. Elizabeth Haynes was delighted at the idea of company. Usually, once winter left its first snowfall, there was little likelihood of seeing another woman's face until spring's thaw.

Only the Paige, Read, Whitney, and Haynes families were present, but with their assorted children and a few grandparents, there were 20 worshippers altogether. The Andersons' baby had the croup, so they could not attend, nor could the Tollivers, whose horse had gone lame two days before. Both families were remembered in prayer.

Nathaniel's strong baritone led the group in several hymns, accompanied by Elizabeth on the out-of-tune piano brought across the ocean by her mother years ago. They had no hymnbooks, but they all knew the words by heart from family services that, until now, had been their only way of fulfilling their religious needs. Once in a while, a circuit preacher might happen by, but that was an unlikely event in such scattered homes.

Nathaniel's sermon, which he had worked on for days, was listened to intently. Even the children, in awe of being allowed the luxury of a morning off from schooling and chores, sat still and good in their very best clothes, most of which had been specially made for this occasion. Elizabeth's eyes were filled with pride as she watched her husband hold his audience so rapt.

She was almost disappointed when Helen Read volunteered her home for the next service, which would be Christmas Sunday, two days before the blessed day. She was sure that Aaron Read would not have the way with words that *her* husband did, but she thought it prudent not to entertain such prideful thoughts. It would certainly be nice to get out of her four-room farmhouse, spacious though it was by comparative standards. The Reads' cabin had only one room. It could hold the group snuggly in front of the big stone fireplace but... there would be no piano.

By 1727, the congregation was established enough to have a name — The Greenfield Fellowship Church — and to begin thinking of constructing a church building. Nathaniel deeded acreage in his East meadow, and logs were cut in the spring. Each man gave what time he could spare to the project, so that it was nearly three years before the 172' x 24' structure was completed. To all, it was a labor of love. Its block-like appearance was relieved by the rise of a small, but definite, steeple, and the first coat of white paint rendered it beautiful in their eyes.

With mixed feelings, Elizabeth supervised the moving of her beloved piano into the church. She was proud to donate it but already missed the momentary release from a hard life that playing music always gave her. Still, she would continue to feel its keys every Sunday, and perhaps she'd find a few minutes for practice during her busy week.

The next challenge was to find a minister for their lovely, new church. Ministers were a scarce commodity, and larger and wealthier communities got first choice. Even though they now numbered 15 spiritually committed families, the financial offerings were sporadic and sparse. If there had been an early snowfall or a dry spring, no one had money for anything but his own family's life necessities. But the sharing of the pulpit by the church members, while economical, left a lot to be desired in spiritual enlightenment.

Then, in 1730, God sent them Alexander Goodwin, a circuit preacher's son who did not relish the travelling life for himself. With very little persuasion, he accepted the call of the Greenfield Fellowship Church. He stayed with the Haynes family until his own cabin was completed, moving into it immediately following his wedding to Marcia Haynes, the first official wedding under the new church roof.

Forty years passed before Alexander and Marcia went to meet the Lord they had so dedicatedly served. The reins of the church were then handed over to Rev. Jeremiah Goodwinter, the son of a preacher in neighboring Enterbury.

And so it went. The church had a life of its own now. None of the founders were alive to see it burn to the ground in 1840, but from the ashes rose a larger and stronger building, similar in style to its predecessor, but with an elevated podium for the preacher, Rev. Doolittle. There was even a stained glass window, the pieces of which had been carefully transported from a glassmaker's shop in Boston.

In time, Greenfield became able to support a Catholic church, and then a Lutheran. The Greenfield Fellowship Church continued to flourish, and in 1980, it stood in the exact center of town. Its majestic steeple had bell chimes now, and they sent forth music for all to hear on Sunday mornings.

Numb

Janette van de Geest Van Gruisen

I came out by a pond —
a perfect round, frozen deep —
and I had to kneel down in the snow,
not to pray, or weep,
but to find the cold,
to touch the crusted snow
with my fingertips,
smooth it like a cheek,
then dig my hands in
and hold them there
until I choked on feeling cold,
because I hadn't felt —
even cold —
for such a long time.

from A Circle of Three: Book of Newport

A. Valentine Smith

Prologue

Mandy can hear the muted shouting of her friends and the adults from the fog-shrouded beach, the setting sun a mere pink glow on the suspended droplets. She's too exhausted from treading cold water to respond. The misty fog feels strange: evil, draining, cold. Her mouth dips below the waterline again. Mandy tries to shut it quickly, but some salty water still gets in. A bit of furious kicking, and her mouth breaks above the waterline again. Gasping and choking, she spits the sea out.

Tired. So tired. The soft shouts seem so far away. *I can't keep treading water.* Her arms and legs feel like lead. A cramp. Her leg. Her left leg is tight and hurts. She's kicking with one leg now. That leg gives out. Mandy is exhausted. She holds her breath as her head slips under. The shoreline shouts become muffled by the seawater.

Mandy raises her arms above her head. She points them toward the bright light dancing on the water's surface. *Bright light? The fog should be blocking the sun. Is this what dying is like?* Little bubbles start to escape the corners of her mouth. A slash of darkness tears across the bright light.

Memories... how it all began... all Mandy has right now.

Elsewhere

B.E. Delaplain

What takes me elsewhere when I am here?
  I feel the warm Pacific as I stroll along the strand
  ebbing evening tides pull me, Elsewhere
  to carefree sun-filled days catching wild Atlantic rollers
    meeting challenges of life with energy, laughter, delight.
Now on this side of the continent so many years gone by
I am at peace with gentler waves
that give serenity to my life.

  I wander past a fence entwined with scarlet blooms
  perfumed bull-blown roses pull me, Elsewhere
  to hollyhocks and daisy chains and chatter in tiny rooms
    middle child of many I stood my ground, certain I was right.
Now on this side of the continent so many years gone by
I am at peace with the compromise
that gives serenity to my life.

  Two boys, one girl with auburn hair frolic with a kite
  sight and breezes seize my heart to pull me, Elsewhere
  I quelled their fears of atomic bombs in a world of senseless wars
    then in silence ached as they scattered to live their separate lives.
Now on this side of the continent so many years gone by
I am at peace with remembrances
that give serenity to my life.

I hear the Universe's song of glory to a rising moon
the majesty of a star-pierced sky lures me, Elsewhere
his voice through romantic nights glimmered with promised dreams
death severed us, no comfort found except the inner spirit as a guide.
Now on this side of the continent so many years gone by
I am at peace knowing there is but Now
and the serenity in my life.

Melissa Martin Ellis

On the Mainland

49
from *Pedestrian Crossing, A Novel*
Janette van de Geest Van Gruisen

52
Vituperative
Gary Bolstridge

53
I-Roc, Do You?
Gary Bolstridge

55
A The Bronwyn *Tale*
Andrew McNabb

61
Battles & Wars
Zona Douthit

65
from *Dishonorable Intentions*
Anne DuBose Joslin

71
The Maypole
Christine L. Mullen

73
Review: *The Noonday Demon:
An Atlas of Depression*
Len DeAngelis

83
The Rider
Gary Bolstridge

from Pedestrian
Crossing, A Novel

Janette van de Geest
Van Gruisen

I am not from here. You might tell, from my appearance or my voice, that I am from another place, perhaps from another time. I come from a place of endless rain and darker skies than you know here. I come from a place where sunshine is a myth, a fairy tale we tell our children so they might think that darkness is not all there is. But how cruel to tell them, you say, when all we can give them is the myth, without a thing to carry in their hand. Well, who can hold sunshine in his hand? Not even you, who have so much of it: can you wake in the morning and capture a day's supply, mold it, hold and make it yours? No, and nor can our children, beneath their dark sky, but here we have been given an unholy gift for words because with them we must create so much that we do not start out with. So we give our children light and blue and gold and liquid words, and they take them from us and make their stories, each child's quite his own.

No, we are not cruel because we are giving all we have. It is not much, but we find, on the whole, it is almost as much as we need. Except for a few of us, who will always go hungry. For us, a thousand colored words are not enough; not for those like me who, despite our fear that we will never find enough, still leave to go in search of more, of more than words, in search of something beyond darkness, dreams, and myths. We leave the familiar territory of deprivation and risk finding disappointment. But we leave. And those we leave behind? Some laugh, some love us for our courage, but mostly they just wave and turn away, back to their storytelling, back to their peculiar understanding of enough, of subsistence.

I am from there. I have tried to be from here, to live in your new perspective, but it eludes me still, after all these years.

I am one of three. The others lived with enough, or so they thought. I was the one who left them behind in what they knew as comfort. The middle one found out late that when comfort is thin it wears out sooner than it is outworn. She wants to leave now but cannot — she is in too deep. She made her bed with a thin coverlet, and into it children came and tied her heart to theirs, though her head and feet still roam, mostly in her dreams. It is too late for her, and I believe she knows it. Her core is dank and bitter now, despite the crisp sweetness of her children's love. She has run out of fairy-tales, exhausted every myth, and has taken now to telling lies instead, at least to herself. What was once enough is no longer.

But I want you to know that it was not always dark where I come from. Long ago, before my time, there was a wealth of sunshine; there were green meadows, primroses on riverbanks, and the song of poor children dancing on brick streets.

I know these things not innately, but from knowledge imparted to me, and this was the reason for my leaving. The mother who made me told me of these things as if they existed only once, in a time that can never return, as if these scenes were frozen forever on a two-dimensional landscape that even the fiercest will could not restore to life. But somewhere beyond that landscape, I have since walked barefoot in those green meadows, seen primroses growing, and heard poor children singing loudly in the street, watched them dancing ever higher. That is why I left.

In the time before I left, no one expected that I would go, although I was born on a Thursday, and so it might have been predicted that I would travel far. But I was tiny and timid and so afraid of the dark all around that it took many silent years to gather the courage to open my eyes and see that there was indeed a door opening outward. It seemed the first few times I tried it there was another hand against the knob, holding me back. But too late, because now that I knew the door existed, I would find a way to pass through it. By that time, I had found a friend:

Gordon had entered my life. "Jump," he said, and he held my hand as, like two ghosts, we went blinking into the light, yet not disappearing, finding form and substance instead of evaporating. Perhaps we have never truly come to trust the light, or to believe in luck, for together, twenty years later, we still hold on to each other when the clouds eclipse the sun or the rains beat down or the electricity fails.

The door we stepped through slammed tightly behind us, and if we had wanted to shelter in it for a while as we surveyed the scene before us, the opportunity was not there. We had arrived in a bright and glaring place and were engulfed in a world of breathless heat, unworldly blossoms, the shrill of tin calypso, smiling toothless taxi drivers, and carnival food that was cooked in no mother's kitchen.

Quite by accident, we lived amid this noise and heat and ribald color for a decade before we felt strong enough to move on, to leave the warmth behind. We swam with sparkling fishes for so long before we were sated with sun and lotuses. From the place of our childhood we had inherited disquiet, the promise of more. We wanted to know seasons, to feel the cold, to wake up from the numbness of unending ease and comfort. We wanted to grow up, grow old, to die living. But first we had to bleed.

Vituperative

Gary Bolstridge

I cannot see
Darkness engulfs me
Eyes fill with tears
I cannot hear
It's the sound of fear

My heart is broken
From words you have spoken
Unlimited joy has turned
To a love spurned
The Wheel Of Life has learned

No secret did I withhold
Yours cannot be told
Trust which would unfold
Once spoken so bold
Is now put on hold

Promise and hope have flown
From the seeds you have sown
The past is in doubt
A future is ruled out
The present hurts

I-Roc, Do You?

Gary Bolstridge

There is always a contingent of people who will pleasantly say "Hello" but will not engage you in conversation. Sometimes this is a good thing. Some of my coworkers see me as a wimpy hippy. I am guilty of the "hippy" tag. True, I don't have the deepest of voice, I cannot recite any sports statistics, and I did not enjoy the movie "Dumb and Dumber." But does that make me a wimp? Apparently it does enough to keep some guys at a distance.

I drive an old Chevy Blazer that has seen better days and straighter bumpers. A few mild dents and 160,000 miles on the odometer announce that I am not a very car-image individual. The Blazer doesn't like to be driven on the highway at high speeds; in fact, it refuses to go over 60, even downhill. It's a senior citizen and just as irascible, but it gets me there and back. I respect that.

One week my Blazer was being repaired, so I had to borrow my son's car: a Chevy Camaro I-Roc — a real muscle car. In fact, you have to be strong just to close the door. The car is so low to the ground that it hurts my arthritic knees to climb in and out of it. I couldn't see where the front of the car ended beyond the hood. There was this vast horizon that I kept staring at and driving toward without ever reaching the Promised Land.

The first day that I drove the I-Roc to work, I was afraid to go over my routine 35 miles per hour. By the third day, I couldn't do under 35. The thing just wouldn't go slow!

Seeing my new ride in the parking lot at work, a few of the guys who'd had minimal contact with me in the past began to ask questions.

"Is it a 5.7 liter, 350 cubic inch, tune port injected engine? Does it handle well? You got low profile, wide tread tires on polished aluminum sport wheels? A 323:1 gear ratio, 4-speed over-drive tranny with a positraction rear end?"

Fearing I would have to explain what the car did have (and not having a clue what that might be!), I answered enthusiastically, "Oh yeah, man. She's got some gitty-up!!" As it turns out, it does have all the things they described. They related to me personal incidents with their Porsches and Corvettes. I had become an unspoken member of their elite club, welcomed into their fold, but I was never very comfortable. The values they ascribed to their machines just didn't matter to me.

By the end of the week, my Blazer was repaired, and I was back to driving it to work. After experiencing the youth of my son's car, the Blazer felt like the senior citizen that it is, and I was back to my normal 35 miles per hour routine. Gradually my newfound friends returned to the distance of our earlier silence. First, just a nod and a "How ya doin'?" rapidly deteriorated to "humph" as we passed each other in the halls. Finally, we were back to avoiding eye contact, and things had returned to normal. Sometimes this is a good thing.

A *The Bronwyn* Tale

Andrew McNabb

Bixby had never dreamed that a building could provide everlasting peace, but the The Bronwyn was not just any building. It was the tallest residential tower anywhere in the world, and as if that were not enough, it provided service that rivaled that of the world's finest five-star hotels.

It was a year ago that he'd first seen the advertisement:

> *The Bronwyn. The Tallest Residential Tower Anywhere in the World. It's not Just Tallest, it's Plushest, too. Never Before Have Unsurpassed Height and Five-Star Comfort been Combined in a Residence. Come with Us. Embark on a Lifelong Vacation.*

Bixby was wealthy. He was first to buy, and the The Bronwyn was now nearly completed. He'd stuck it out in his old apartment for as long as he could, but the allure of height and service unsurpassed had proved overwhelming. He'd decided six months ago that, if he couldn't yet partake of it, he could at least be near it. He'd been living in the park across the street ever since.

His hair had grown long, a tangled beard hung from his face. His clothes smelled of pigeon poo and dirt, but Bixby didn't mind because when opening day arrived he would clean himself in a bathroom *"so deluxe, so full of soothing comforts, the body would leave refreshed, as if granted new skin.*" He'd memorized those words and others from the brochure that had served as friend and map. He quoted from it when times got tough, when the days were long and the nights even longer, taking comfort in the descriptions of the many firsts, the countless never-befores he'd soon experience. And each night before bed, he whispered to himself the building motto: *The Bronwyn. The embodiment of all that life can be — and can't.*

And now, from his bench in the balmy city evening, Bixby looked up into the oncoming darkness, to the blacked-out spot in the sky above all other buildings — residential and commercial — that was the rising The Bronwyn. He focused on a lighted window and pictured himself behind it. Tomorrow was opening day, and he would stand in his own lighted window, enmeshed in comfort, looking out at the left-behind place called earth, partaking of what life can be — and can't.

It was barely dawn when Bixby marched across the The Bronwyn plaza. A white-gloved doorman stood inside the polished doors. Their eyes met, and though Bixby smiled, the doorman looked right through him. When Bixby didn't retreat, the doorman stepped outside.

"What is it?"

"Um," replied Bixby, taken aback. That didn't sound like a five-star greeting. "I have an apartment..."

"Today is opening day. We have no need for your kind around here. Now scoot."

His kind? What did that mean? Was he in the right place? He looked up into the sky. The building top swayed in atmospheric splendor. Yes, this was most definitely the The Bronwyn. *See our tower poke the sky.* But this wasn't the embodiment of five-star service. And he most definitely didn't feel as if he had embarked on a lifelong vacation. It wasn't supposed to be like this.

The doorman stepped back inside. A panel of glass between them, Bixby's dream was slipping away. What to do? He tinkled his fingers together in panic. He approached the door. The doorman once again stepped out.

"I said 'Away.'" He brushed his hand through the air.

"This is not five-star service!" cried Bixby. Sickness rolled in his stomach; even if things worked out now, the experience was tainted. There was no imperfection in ultimate peace! And if this was ultimate peace, thought Bixby, then... the implications were unthinkable.

With a flash of clarity, a solution emerged. There was a magic phrase, an antidote to poor service. "I'd like to speak with the manager," he blurted. And wanting nothing more than to begin again, he added, "He can find me over there, on a bench in the park across the street."

Bixby sat on a bench that provided a good view of the building entrance. Though the morning was bright with mid-summer sun, he could still see the impressive twinkle of the lobby's twin chandeliers. *Biggest, twinkliest chandeliers. Never have two chandeliers of this size been grouped together in one location. All for your bright pleasure.* With each subtle movement around the The Bronwyn's doors, Bixby's heart leaped as he waited for the manager to emerge, to set matters straight.

Hours passed. No one emerged. Bixby replayed the episode over and over in his mind, each time returning to the same conclusion, seeing no other way to have handled it. Wasn't that what one was supposed to do, ask for the manager? It was all too much, he thought, how could it have even gotten to that point? This was the The Bronwyn. It was the ultimate in peace. They'd said so, and he believed them. And now, feeling betrayed, Bixby reached for the brochure and turned to page one.

> *Mission Statement: Our goal is to provide our resident-guests with a living environment that exceeds those provided by the worlds finest five-star hotels. We will do this through the combination of physical environment — plushness encased by height unsurpassed — and service heretofore unknown. Our residents-guests' unlimited, unburdened happiness is our only desire.*

Underneath the statement was a picture of a man smiling peacefully, no doubt from service heretofore unknown. Bixby exhaled deeply. Reassured, he was certain the manager wouldn't be long. But how long was five-star-service long?

Morning passed. The manager hadn't emerged. Curiously, there had been no activity at all. The doorman simply waited at attention behind his door, exiting occasionally to polish the window or gather a piece of dust.

Afternoon arrived. The sun beat relentlessly down. Yet Bixby waited quietly, staring into the plaza's fountain, mesmerized. *Ours is a spring water fountain. Sip from the pure goodness, or look down on it from up high. It's your choice. Nothing less will do.* And Bixby thirsted.

Finally, in the early evening, there was movement. A handful of people exited the building; building employees, Bixby surmised, by their joyful demeanor, their flawless posture. His heart pulsed. Was the manager in their ranks? Would his wait be over?

But no one broke free or even looked in his direction. Instead, the employees arranged themselves in a line. And then, seemingly on cue, a procession of limousines pulled into the looping driveway. Doors opened. Stepping from cars were people Bixby recognized from the brochure. Yes, there was the couple in evening dress from page two, he with sophisticated gray hair, she with timeless beauty; *Dine in our very own five-star restaurant.* And there was the successful businessman from page three; *All deals are complete at The Bronwyn.* And the man with perfectly sculpted muscles from page six; *State of the art fitness facilities. We've got it all!* And others, too many to all be from the brochure, but to Bixby, looking like they very well could be.

They were handed glasses of champagne. A speech was made. By the manager? Bixby's view was obstructed by a waving flag. He stepped up on the bench to get a better look. What was he saying? His ears longed for a soothing five-star speech.

Then, to great applause, the doors opened! The doorman bowed at the waist, maintaining his position as resident-guests hurried through. Bixby clamored to be among their ranks as he watched the bodies scuttle across the lobby. *Never has so much Imperador marble been laid in one contiguous area.* And he watched them disappear into open elevators so numerous that no one had to wait.

And where was the manager? Bixby looked about the driveway, the entrance to the park: no one. His attention was drawn back to the building. His head tilted to take in the sky. One by one the compartments lit up. Darkened bodies appeared in windows. Motionless, they looked out over the city; to Bixby, all the way to Heaven.

It was now fully dark. There was no activity at the bottom of the building. No one arrived. No one left. But Bixby refused to panic, determining it was perfectly logical, this. His situation, he realized, was "out-of-building." The resident-guests on the inside required assistance, and their needs took precedence. Right about now, he guessed, the manager was engaged, walking from one distinguished residence to the next, welcoming the new resident-guests. Little comforts they needed, and explanations as to how things worked. After all, there was much inside that man had never experienced. Oh, thought Bixby, it will be so good to finally be there!

All of the excitement had taken its toll. Exhaustion took hold. Bixby lay down on the bench and looked high into the The Bronwyn sky. He focused on a body standing in a lighted window. So still was the man. He put himself in that man's body, hoping to feel his peace, deciding that one more night in the park wouldn't hurt. And besides, five-star service would surely respond within twenty-four hours. His eyes grew heavy.

Shortly after dawn, Bixby was awakened by a human presence. "Pleased to meet you!" he exclaimed, standing up, extending a hand. But there was no hand there to receive him. There was a man, however, slumped over on a bench a short distance away.

Was he the manager? An emissary? Bixby couldn't be sure. If he were, wouldn't he have woken him up? But wait a second, he told himself, perhaps five-star service had been employed. Perhaps the man had seen him sleeping and decided not to wake him. Sleep, after all, was a great indulgence, and being woken from it was often jarring and unpleasant and surely not aligned with five-star pleasure. Oh, how they think of everything!

Bixby studied the man. Poor fellow. Tired from a night of providing service. How draining it must be! But what should he do? Wake him?

No! Heel! He pinched himself on the inner thigh for even considering it. After all, the man had let him sleep. He was no better than the man.

Ashamed, he knew that the man hadn't asked himself such a question, and if the man had let him sleep, well then he would let the man sleep. And so it was settled.

When hours passed and the man didn't wake, Bixby grew anxious. He looked up, to the building. The sun once again pounded his head, and he wanted nothing more than to pull from his body the ragged clothes that clung to his itchy, dirty skin. Why did things never work out for him? Peace was just a building away. If he could only get there, it would all be over. And this man! This man! How, after all these hours, was he still asleep? Snoring, no less, with such incredible vigor that it appeared he was somehow faking!

"Don't ruin it!" he chided himself. "He will wake. He will wake. A man can't sleep forever."

So Bixby sat down on his bench. He looked once again to the sky and admired the tallest and plushest residential tower anywhere in the world and dreamed of himself inside. He stayed that way for a very long time. Every so often looking over to the man on the bench, wondering if he should shift him — the hot summer sun was baking his sleeping face. And that was not five-star.

Battles & Wars

Zona Douthit

In 1954, the whole family lived in a big white house with green shutters on Riverside Drive. The house sat proudly in a row of stately homes, some of the best in town.

Nineteen fifty-four was also the year World War II caught up with the entire family, even though the little kids, Tommy and Patty, hadn't been born until after the war. But by 1954, the demons from the Japanese POW camp overtook Dad and shot to hell his bayonet-sharp Marine facade. One Friday night, with the dining room table set for dinner and the little kids watching Mickey Mouse Club in the front room, Bataan came to life again in the foyer next to the Wurlitzer jukebox. Dad punched Mom in the face and broke her nose as she walked through the front door half an hour late, then he started up the stairs to get his gun to "finish the job."

It was only the aroma of pot roast that had kept the three, pre-war teenage sons home for dinner on a Friday. There was a school dance that night. If that pot roast hadn't tempted them, they might've just grabbed a burger at the drive-in where the girls skated out to the cars to take orders. But they were home, combing hair into perfect ducktails, teasing the little kids, listening to a Buddy Holly 45. They saved Mom's life, maybe even the little kids' lives.

It wasn't easy. All three of them were bruised for a week after the battle with Dad because Dad was fighting Jap demons, and they were just scared boys protecting their mother. Dad was a big man with a barrel chest that proudly displayed all of his war medals when he wore his uniform. The teenage sons were a tall, skinny lot. It took all three of them to drag him off the stairs and out of the house. Dad was never allowed back in.

The next year the oldest son joined the Marine Corps and would never live with the family again. They moved into a smaller house: three bedrooms, no dining room. It was the last house on the street before the mill. The composition siding was a bilish yellow that matched the smell of the sulfur smoke from the mill. Across the street was an abandoned Victorian house. The constant rain had washed it bare of paint. The little kids, Tommy and Patty, hunted for ghosts in it.

By 1956, the second son had joined up, and the remnants of the family moved again, this time to a five-room cottage on the other side of town. Train tracks ran down the middle of the street, and when the trains came by twice a day, the little house rattled as if its dentures were loose. Dad got transferred to Camp Pendelton. Before he left, he signed up the third son, who would get a GED later. Now only Mom and the little kids weren't in the Marine Corps, at least not any more.

The little house had a yard on the side with a picket fence, but no one mowed the grass. Patty was ashamed about the grass, but no one ever talked about it. Mom worked as a secretary for $400 a month and drove a '49 Hudson that broke down weekly. No one ever talked about the lack of a man to take care of the car and the grass. Patty was only nine, but Tommy was eleven by then. He could've mowed the grass, but he was so angry all the time that Mom just didn't have the energy to fight with him about it. Besides, he was repeating the fourth grade. She didn't ask too much of him.

Tommy and Patty were on their own after school. Mom's only rule was that they stick together. Tommy and Patty usually stayed away from the river. It wasn't that Mom had warned them so much as that the river was dark and murky, and when the tide was out, the exposed mud flats smelled like the big, eviscerated river rat the cat had left on the porch one morning with the milk bottles. Patty was afraid of the river after that, and while Tommy was fearless and would go anywhere, he usually found things for them to do away from the river. Throughout the autumn they had explored the golden alders and loden green cedars and picked blackberries on the ridge behind the school. During the wet winter they had played Monopoly and Parcheesi at home. A false spring day came in February when it wasn't raining, but it was too muddy to get up to the ridge. Tommy needed adventure. He wanted to explore the old wharf behind the train turntable. Patty was ashamed to be afraid in the face of Tommy's perpetual courage, so eventually she gave in.

They tightrope-walked the tracks about a half-mile, past the turntable, past the paint-naked warehouse that hadn't been used for decades. The wharf was rough-hewn planks, some still held in place by square-headed, rusty nails, some not. Huge logs, eight feet across that must have come from the first cut of the forests at the turn of the century still anchored the wharf into the deep silt. The old logs had stood in the river so long they had sucked up the river's boggy color. At high tide, the wharf was barely distinguishable from the water.

By the time Tommy and Patty got to the wharf, deep gray clouds had scudded across the sun. What had been a spring breeze was now winter gusts. Patty was only wearing a green cardigan over a short-sleeved Peter Pan blouse and yellow, corduroy pedal pushers. She wanted to turn back.

"We're here now." Tommy looked at her like she was a dumb girl.

The wood looked rotten. She didn't like the river's being so high. Where did the rats go when the water was high? Tommy pointed out that there were three other boys on the wharf. It had to be okay.

Patty followed him out about half way. The three boys at the end of the wharf were hunched together. They were bigger than Tommy, maybe sixth graders. They looked up. That's when Patty refused to go a step farther. Tommy went out and said something to them. The boys laughed in a way that made Patty want to go home. Tommy threw a stick into the river. One of the older boys offered Tommy a cigarette. Tommy glanced at Patty then took it. He put it between his lips like he had seen the older brothers do, but he didn't suck in.

One of the sixth graders walked toward Patty. "I got something for you, too."

Patty was used to teasing. Her older brothers teased her all the time. Dad said you can only be teased if you want to be teased. Patty stood very still and tried not to want to be teased.

The other two boys trailed along after the first. Tommy watched from the end of the wharf, cigarette smoke whipping around his hand. Suddenly, the three boys were all around her and she couldn't see Tommy anymore. Then one of them moved as fast as darkness came when a light was switched off. He yanked down her yellow corduroy pedal pushers and her panties with little blue flowers. A cutting wind rushed from behind her and between her bare legs. She shivered; the sixth grade boys laughed and pointed at her little-girl nakedness.

The sinister snickers were still echoing over the river when Tommy pulled her away. She wanted to stop and make him beat them up. That's what he should do: beat them up. Only violence could cancel her shame. But he just said quietly that it was time to go home.

They never told Mom and never talked about it. It was like the night Dad fought demon Japs in the front hall. But Patty was mad. Tommy was supposed to protect her. For a lot of years, she kept the image in her mind like a dog-eared photograph in her wallet of Tommy beating those boys and throwing them into the muddy river.

Forty years later on a long car trip, Tom told her how scared he had been hanging out of the back of chopper spraying the Vietnamese jungle with automatic weapon fire, not seeing who or what he might've killed. He talked about how the marijuana and tequila had dulled the memories for twenty-five years, how he ran guns into and dope out of places where they spoke Spanish just so he didn't have to find a home, how he had looked for God on channel 18, even sent a hundred dollars to the post office box on the screen.

That afternoon, Pat decided not to leave her third husband. It was time she stopped expecting so much of men. She wished she had beaten up those sixth grade boys herself.

from Dishonorable Intentions

Anne DuBose Joslin

L ooking back over the previous fourteen months in the presidential campaign, I felt as if I had been on a non-stop roller coaster. Bush was down in the fall of 1987; he was ahead by year's end; he was crushed in Iowa; he was a wimp; he would never win over a heavyweight like Bob Dole; the vice president's political career was over. Then, Bush rebounded in the New Hampshire primary. He won! We won! After Super Tuesday, we knew that Bush was going to be the Republican nominee and thought he might be up against the leading Democrat at the time, Al Gore. A few weeks later, it looked as if Jesse Jackson was going to be his opponent. During four long months in the spring and early summer, it looked as if there were no way Bush could pull ahead of any Democrat by November. Our thoughts were confirmed in July, just before the Democratic Convention, when the campaign staff was sure that Dukakis had it locked up. In mid-August, Bush had been the underdog by seventeen points, struggling for recognition in a race that seemed already over. California was predicted to throw its huge block of 47 electoral votes to Dukakis. The press and the polls said there was no way. It was over. Added to everything else, Bush had been hit with the "Quayle thing." It all seemed so hopeless... until September, when Dukakis dropped the ball and left an opening for Bush not only to catch up but to pass him by. Did Bush actually have a chance of winning?!

The moment Dukakis started to flounder, the Bush campaign members were there to take advantage of the unexpected opportunity.

The anti-Dukakis publicity that Baker and Atwater and Ailes and Pinkerton used during the summer months — advertisements predicted to be out-dated by summer's end — lived on into the fall, never losing their punch. *Dukakis* turned out to be "the issue," not Bush, leaving *Dukakis* to defend his position, not Bush.

The Dukakis strike squad had launched just as many attacks on Bush (Iran-Contra, Noriega, and the environment) as the Bush team had discharged on Dukakis, and they were just as negative — just not as effective. As always, the top Bush media guru, Roger Ailes, a master of his craft, had been brilliant in his use of advertising images. Just the right ones, delivered at just the right time. That was not by coincidence; that was the mark of a true professional.

The journalists of 1988 had coined the phrase "negative campaigning," but neither camp could really be labeled "unfair"; they pretty much kept to public record and political philosophy. Bush insisted on that course, and I believe Dukakis did as well. To my knowledge, the commercials produced in 1988 by the Bush media experts — including the furlough, the flag, and the harbor — were accomplished in a proficient and skillful manner. The research material was accurate, and the sourcing ethical. Upon reflection, I wished that instead of laboring incognito on my campaign craft (researching Boston Harbor), I could have had the opportunity to work directly with the master himself.

As the final weeks of the campaign rolled on, and still relying on the summer attack ads to be effective, the Bush team simply sat back and watched its candidate spin into the winner's seat. At this point, the only necessary strategy was to keep doing what they already were doing: replaying the commercials and then replaying them again. The tactic was working without needing to be refueled. Without effort. It was like a surfer's perfect wave caught at the perfect moment. The one that, with a thrust and momentum all its own, takes the rider safely to shore. All he has to do is remain onboard.

On the day of the election, after a volatile last week on the stump and a grueling last weekend of whistle-stop campaigning, Dukakis finally was back in Brookline, and Bush was in Houston. It was Tuesday, November 8. The power-driven campaign machine came to an abrupt halt. The strategists, spin weavers, and schedulers; the pollsters, advertising sages, and ghost writers; as well as the press agents, media mongers, researchers, and candidates all stopped and put their tasks aside. Baker, Atwater, Brady, Teeter, Fuller, Spencer, and Darman closed shop. As for those of us in Washington, including hundreds of Bush campaign workers, spouses, escorts, and families, we gathered for a victory party on election evening. Dan and Marilyn Quayle joined us at the Washington Hilton Hotel.

When the major television networks declared Bush the winner (with the exit-poll projection of more than 270 electoral votes), the usually sedate ballroom at the Hilton, filled with women wearing shimmering cocktail dresses and men in dark suits, turned into a circus scene. While the victor's song was being sung and the champagne flowed, we celebrated a conquest that just two months earlier could not have been foreseen.

As masters of the universe, we marveled at our splendid political strategy, forgetting about the claims from the press of having run a campaign that was "issueless" and having conducted ourselves in an "unworthy" manner. That night in the Hilton, the campaign staff chose to believe that the issues had been real and that the Bush victory represented a well-informed choice of the American people.

Although it had not been a landslide, and the Republicans lost seats in both the House and the Senate, making for another Democratic Congress, Bush swept every region in the country and won by more than 7 million votes. With 426 electoral votes, he had a hefty advantage on Dukakis, who totaled only 111. From an estimated 94 million voters, Bush obtained 54% of the popular vote and Dukakis received 46%. (The presidency had not been won by a popular-vote loser since 1888, 100 years earlier.)

Until just weeks before, it was a feat no one — not even the ultimate campaign manager, Lee Atwater — had forecast. Although Atwater always said, "We will win!" most of us realized he was saying that to stay optimistic during the rough times — all those nights and days and days and nights that had pretty much made up five of the past seven months. The vice president had been guaranteed to lose. In spite of that politically astute assurance, Mr. Bush had won.

George Bush's triumph, though significant, was a fluke. Yes, we had successfully attacked Dukakis, but our opponent simply had not responded. Truth be told, the Bush campaign had won on luck more than anything. Not the most noble way to win a political battle, but that's the way it was. Having said that, I give Bush, Ailes, and Atwater credit where credit is due. Bush was an honorable candidate, Ailes a sensational media artist, and without Atwater, we may have lost even with the last-minute advantage. Nonetheless, it had been the mistakes of the Dukakis team, both in the offensive and defensive lines, that had delivered Bush the crown of victory on Tuesday November 8, 1988, and, subsequently, made him the 41st President of the United States of America.

The day after the election was declared a holiday for all Republican National Committee and Campaign staff. I was invited to Andrews Air Force Base for the arrival ceremony, in honor of the Bushes, who were flying back to Washington D.C. from Houston.

My former office-mate in research at headquarters, Russell Rockwell, asked me to ride to Andrews with him and his wife. Russell had been the only one at the campaign to keep in touch with me after my "leaving" the research staff and joining the Republican Committee. He had extended to me an invitation to visit their Pennsylvania country home anytime I needed to get away. I was then, and always will be, grateful for my friendship with the Rockwells, who today remain the same warm and gracious "associates" whom I met on the campaign trail over a decade ago. On the morning of the President-elect's return to the Capital City, the Rockwells and I jubilantly left the District and headed en route for Andrews.

The crowd on hand was small in comparison with the one at the Victory Ball the night before and, for that reason, seemed much more personal and less remote from the nominee-turned-winner. I liked the feeling of closeness — as if I were part of a large family in which one of the members had just won a stupendous award. Vicariously, I experienced the moment as my victory, too.

The hangar that usually housed the president's Air Force One had been transformed into an arrival site and greeting area. Bleachers filled the space in which sleek presidential jets usually parked. Out on the tarmac, the imposing Boeing 707, flying the Bushes home, made a smooth landing. The plane, with a football-field-length fuselage painted white and an under-belly in blue, slowly taxied toward the hangar in which we were seated. I could see on the upper portion of Air Force Two the words "The United States of America" distinctly written in bold, jet-black letters; the American flag was emblazoned on the tail, with the numbers "56974" inscribed directly underneath the red, white, and blue flag.

Upon arriving at Andrews, I had been given, as had the other guests, a small American flag, to be waved when the Bushes and Quayles appeared. When the foursome finally did deplane Air Force Two, hundreds of flags went into the air, along with a multitude of cheers. It may sound like a cliché, but at that moment, I felt overwhelmingly proud to be an American. On that unusually warm November afternoon, as I waved my flag, I wished that my Father — maybe in his Navy dress blues — could have been standing there beside me in all his 6-foot 4-inch glory. Father, the patriot, coming from five generations of military loyalists, would have known exactly how I felt and been pleased. Upon his seeing the next commander-in-chief looking so vibrant and ready to assume command of "the troops," Father would have experienced the moment the same way as I: with joy.

All the disappointments, anger, surprises, and delights that I had undergone in the past fourteen months drifted through me, leaving me with a dual sense of exhaustion and gratitude. He made it! We made it! I made it! I was confident that President-elect Bush would bring with him to the White House the pride, loyalty, and service to country upon which our nation was founded, virtues that I felt he so aptly represented. More than ever, I believed he was the decent, honorable man I thought him to be when I first stepped foot in The Woodward Building in September 1987 to work in his presidential campaign. Now, Bush returned to Washington to claim his prize. He deserved it — the "shining moment" in a year of many blemished ones.

Balloons and American flags covered the makeshift campaign platform adjacent to the mammoth plane, from which George Bush, with Barbara and the Quayles standing next to him, delivered the requisite remarks and congratulations. After Bush thanked us for contributing to his conquest, he paid tribute to Reagan, saying that the former president "was one of the great heroes of the modern era."

Standing amongst the banners and crepe paper, I remembered something Bush had said about himself not so long ago at the Republican Convention in New Orleans, "I may not be the most eloquent. I may sometimes be a little awkward, but there is nothing self-conscious in my love of country." Bush had spoken then, as he did now, as the man — not the man running for office.

George Herbert Walker Bush, who started his presidential campaign amidst charges that he was "too nice" to win, celebrated the fact that he had proven them wrong. His dream of triumph had become a reality. The statesman had won the presidency by a throw of the dice, but nevertheless, it was a lucky pitch, and he had won.

And now he was starting a new game. With the 1988 campaign over, the 73-day transition to take the president-elect to the White House had begun. Forces were presumably already in place to ensure that it happened efficiently and without delay. I would find out sooner than most just how ready they were.

The Maypole
Christine L. Mullen

I hang over the sill of our third-floor tenement on Ladyburn Street. Some folk use a pillow so their ribs don't hurt, but my granny says no one should be hanging out the window that far or that long to need a pillow. Granny would not be pleased to know that I have to stand on the dining room chair to reach the window and I need to climb up on the ledge to unlock and open it. "I'll skin you alive if I catch you climbing up on that window ledge" is what my Mammy says.

The climb skins my chin and bruises my knees. I am strong compared to Cathy Tonner and Jean Kane, who are bigger than me, and I can run faster and push harder while in a queue for rationed sweeties.

Today as I hang out the window, my ribs hurt. There are welcome-home banners hung out second- and third-floor windows, upstairs, across the street, up and down the street. Mrs. Kane and Florrie Hurst's Mammy are trying to connect a third banner between their second-floor windows and are laughing. Daddies are coming home from the war. Francie Donnachie's and Joe Morrison's Daddies came home last week.

When Jean and Rena Kane's Daddy comes home that next day, they don't want to come out and play. So I go into their back green to swing on the maypole their Uncle Danny made from the clothesline. When Uncle Danny is drunk, which is often, he doesn't pay any attention. I know he will not be telling me I can't play on their maypole today. I watch their scullery window to try to catch another glimpse of their Daddy in a soldier's khaki uniform, with his soldier's hat tucked into a shoulder epaulet.

People cry, drink, sing, and talk to friends and strangers, inviting all to share in the festivities. My Mammy tries to laugh and joke with them, but I can tell she is trying too hard. Her iris-blue eyes are still looking at something far away.

Review:
The Noonday Demon:
An Atlas of Depression

Len DeAngelis

Although I bought *The Noonday Demon: An Atlas of Depression,* by Andrew Solomon (Scribner, 2001) soon after its publication, I resisted the reading. I had read both Joyce Carol Oates's review in the June 24, 2001, *The New York Times* and "The Hidden Plague," by Solomon in *Out,* July 2001. I knew the impact of Mr. Solomon's writing. We had swapped emails following the article on his mother's suicide in *The New Yorker* in 1998. Both of our mothers bore two sons; we were each the elder. What Mr. Solomon shared about his mother in *The New Yorker* article, I anticipated about my mother in his book. I wanted to read it in a setting where the topic might be most contrasted, so I took it to Hawaii.

My goal was to savor one of the twelve chapters per day. I boarded the return plane not having read half of the 571 pages. When I landed in Providence, RI, I had five pages left and read them before going to sleep that night. A friend who suffers from depression met me at the airport and heard my reaction to the book on the drive home. She said, "I could have been one of those people he wrote about. I have to wait for the short version. I'd love to read it but don't have the attention span. I don't think I've read two books all the way through since... I can't remember when." She typifies the effort Mr. Solomon exerts communicating for those who are depressed, trying to accomplish what many take for granted in a day. Time, much time, is lost by those who have depression, and search as they may, like Proust, they learn it is lost forever, sometimes, even to memory.

The life of one depressed is uniquely distinguishable and bound with the lives of those around him so that the two elements become a third, like flour and yeast and water becoming dough. Depression strikes all economic classes, though Mr. Solomon becomes an advocate for the economically disadvantaged with depression.

Mr. Solomon has researched his book thoroughly and received the National Book Award for his efforts. As I read the pages, I wondered how much he left out, what notes he had sacrificed because the book was controlling him versus the reverse. Chapters VII, History, and XI, Evolution, I read with less interest than the others but recognize their importance to the author's continuing journey, his roadmap, his atlas, through this affliction. And, there were chapters and stories I finished with disappointment because I wanted to read more of what they offered. For example, Chapter XII on Hope, with its introduction of Angel, can and should be read by non-sufferers with gratitude and by sufferers with relief and prayer.

Mr. Solomon makes frequent literary references, spicing the work with the words of Shakespeare, Dickinson, Keats, Whitman, et al., but the most profound words other than his own are by Angel on p. 425:

> I wish I could cry
> as easy as the sky: The tears don't come
> as easily now. They're
> stuck inside my soul.
>
> It's empty and I am afraid
> Do you feel the emptiness? I guess
> it's my own fear from within. I should
> be brave and battle that fear
> but it's a war that's gone on
> for so damned long. I'm tired.
>
> The children are growing and the tears
> in my eyes are flowing. Missing the
> growth of them is like missing the seasons
> change, missing the roses that bloom
> in spring and missing snowflakes falling
> in winter. How many more years
> do I have to miss? The years won't
> stop for me or for them and why

should they? They will continue to
blossom and
bloom and my life will continue
to stand still like a silent pond.

As I write this, snow squalls.
In the four pages discussing "A Note on Method," Mr. Solomon
writes of the five years it took to write the book and the various twists and
turns he encountered along the way. The author explains, "Writing on
depression is painful, sad, lonely, and stressful. Nonetheless, the idea
that I was doing something that might be useful to others was uplifting;
and my increased knowledge has been useful to me" (13). Cathartic?
No. But here is a spokesman for those who cannot communicate
because depression eats their energy. His credibility is enhanced by his
experiences. Drugs. Sex. Violence. He has lived them and writes about
them personally and generally, striking an enviable balance that keeps
the reader intrigued.

The following chapter synopses are intended to help those, like my
friend, who do not have the attention span to read the book and, even
in small chapter dosages, need a guide, and to encourage readers to
explore the book itself.

Chapter I: Depression

The author defines the term and the origin of depression in the body,
the brain, where chemical imbalances produce depression without one's
control. Depression hits us all differently and in varying degrees. The
distinguishing element is duration: how long a depression lasts
determines whether you suffer from it beyond the expected experiences
of life. The causes remain unknown, and one cannot control one's
thoughts in its midst, yet depression teaches. Mr. Solomon offers a
solution: Love. It sounds natural and agreeable but practicing it is the
challenge.

Chapter II: Breakdowns

Mr. Solomon shares how the order of his life was disrupted by an intruder on "little cat feet," sneaking in like Carl Sandberg's "Fog," a metaphor for the state one experiences. Sometimes there is a forecast, little squalls before the storm. Sometimes there is no warning. There may be fear, abandon, a disintegration of the senses, and anxiety. A lot goes on in a depression, and the author shares the technical aspects of its presence.

Once predisposed to depression, the brain can return to it. What can happen to us physically, with heart damage for example, can happen mentally to our minds, and we need to recognize the significance of that possibility. It may never really leave. It may be triggered. Breakdowns are boxsteps — two forward, one back. It may run in families. It certainly affects families and friends.

This chapter resonated for me because of my mother. I tried to imagine her experiences in the early part of the last century. She was born in 1914 and attempted to share with me some of what she could remember about her breakdowns. In those days, a visiting doctor gave B-12 shots, and no one understood the resistance to life. It was hell. My mother's last breakdown forced my father to agree to electroconvulsive therapy (ECT), shock treatments. I was in the service at the time and agreed that he did not have a choice. Commitment is scary, and caring for her himself strained a difficult relationship between two people who didn't know what was going on. The treatment got her to live with the depression, but the episodes continued in varying degrees until she died in 1980, at age 66, of her first myocardial infarction. Stress was not a descriptor in those days, but I'm sure a factor in her body's dis-ease. She took available medication. She lacked the bootstrap gene and the self-reliance gene.

Now, there is improved medication. When you find it, take it; when it no longer works, find something else and take that and continue the medication, Mr. Solomon advises. You play chemical roulette.

What depression does to a relationship is overwhelming. Between two people, it is an intruder. Among more, it is, in Keats's words, "La Belle Dame Sans Merci," the beautiful lady without mercy. Housewife activity probably preoccupied my mother, so she had no time to entertain the intruder until time allowed. Then, like an unwanted guest, it entered, walking in like the night. "The worst of depression lies in a present moment that cannot escape the past it idealizes or deplores." (99).

Chapter III: Treatments

Mr. Solomon simplifies the treatment therapies into two divisions: talking and physical (which includes medication, electroshock, and ECT). One should complement the other. Consider who coordinates both these treatments. He advises meeting with a therapist whom you like. Of course, this makes sense, but so often, when vulnerable and indecisive and apathetic, we rely on others for decisions. Even under duress our instincts deserve attention.

Solomon discusses cognitive-behavior therapy (CBT) and interpersonal therapy for attaining the best records under talking therapy. On page 111, he cites English professors as helpful as professional therapists because of the quality of human understanding they possess. Teachers of English acquire adjunctive cross-discipline talents for persisting in reading and grading to a degree that other teachers do not. Writing and art can play a role. Side-effects must be considered with medication. Antidepressants affect the phases of sexual experiences; some people experience libido overflow. Viagra helps boost testosterone. Solomon admits to feeling like a dartboard for meds. Researchers are working in four new directions: prevention, specific drugs, faster drugs, and symptom versus biological position.

According to Solomon, the most successful physical treatment is the least clean, ECT, and he presents the procedure. Many want to live without drugs, but throughout the book, Mr. Solomon supports medication. There is a difference between being addictive and being dependent. "Depression is a mental illness. Living with depression is like trying to keep your balance while you dance with a goat." (125). It is like being in a body with an alien director, the brain. He writes sensitively about faith and hope, and his last chapter, on Hope, is a stunner that I call "the Book of the Bible according to the Disciple Andrew Solomon." For one with depression, living is the hardest work of life.

Chapter IV: Alternatives

"Depression is a disease of thought processes and emotions, and if something changes your thought processes and emotions in the correct direction, that qualifies as a cure." (137). Exercise, diet, light boxes, massage, herbs, etc. deserve consideration. Homeopathy and journal writing are discussed within the book's limits. Exercise produces endorphins; energy begets energy, like sugar craves sugar.

Solomon discusses friends and the "buddy system" and support groups. Surgery is a last resort and cingulotomy, in which a hole is drilled in the front of the skull and electrodes destroy brain tissue, results in "no permanent change in memory or cognitive or intellectual function" (164). The author also traveled to West Africa to participate in a ndeup ceremony, an animist ritual that predates voodoo. Gene therapy is remote. Solomon's personal experience bolsters his credibility and adds intrigue to the facts.

Chapter V: Populations

"No two people have the same depression." (173). More women than men suffer from it, which becomes more significant for mothers, with the effect on the mental health of children. Anaclitic depression occurs in young children. They need therapy as depression inhibits personality development. The elderly, African Americans, East Asians, gays, and the Inuits of Greenland, who are sunless for three months a year, each have significant experiences with depression.

Mr. Solomon writes that depression is underestimated in teens. In my 32-plus years in the classroom, I saw teens latching on to labels and letters too easily. Some wore ADD (attention deficit disorder) like a tattoo and with pride. The statement that 50% of high school students have thought about killing themselves makes me wonder, but Solomon documents it on page 461 (George Colt, *The Enigma of Suicide*, p.39). Suicide is discussed in literature and life, and some teens associate with the act when they hear and read of other teens committing suicide. Certainly, once it occurs in a locale, others imitate. For many teens, weighing what is serious and what is fleeting involves miscalculation, and something as serious as suicide deserves investigation regardless of how camouflaged or in what manner — usually "joking" — it surfaces. I think the statistic that is even more crucial about teens is the nearly 100% who don't think that adults listen to them.

Chapter VI: Addiction

Mr. Solomon makes addiction comprehensible. He presents technical terms and may lose readers temporarily in the quality of substance he provides, but it is the simplification of complicated connections that demands that the book be read in its entirety; readers should not feel that a review suffices.

Put simply, addiction takes on a life of its own regardless of how one got there. Self-medication with illicit drugs defeats its purpose because the drug craves more drugs, having inhibited the sensitivity of dopamine receptors (a chemical in the neurotransmitters of the brain). "Depression may be the cause of substance abuse; depression may be the result of substance abuse; depression may alter or exaggerate substance abuse; depression may coexist with substance abuse without affecting it; depression and substance abuse may be two symptoms of a single problem." (221).

Caffeine, nicotine, alcohol, and genes are discussed. Many still believe that marijuana is manageable. However, it is anti-motivational, and its leaves contain 400 identifiable compounds with unknown effects (229). Teens need to know this. Drugs exemplify the "more is less" cliché: the more you want the less pleasure you get. Mr. Solomon gives attention to opiates, hallucinogens, benzos (benzodiazepines — see what I mean about doing his homework?).

Solomon states he is no longer independent, but reliant on drugs — "a cousin of addiction" (237). Drugs may help you tolerate the misery, but medical advice and coordination is essential. As with a therapist, find someone you trust and like.

Chapter VII: Suicide

While discussing this review, a colleague asked me, "How does one survive to write about suicide therapy?"

Depression makes the consideration of suicide prominent. Is suicide a human right? Should people be forced to live against their wills? For every successful suicide there are sixteen attempts (251). "How prone someone is to suicide is determined by personality, genetics, childhood and rearing, alcoholism or substance abuse, chronic illness, and cholesterol level." (253).

Often we cite reason as something that differentiates us from other animals. Suicide is also a differentiation. "Suicide is chronically underreported." (259). Though he admires his mother for her suicide in 1991 (ovarian cancer) and wrote about it in *The New Yorker,* in 1998, he cites it as "the cataclysm of my life" (268). As scary as suicide may be, for some, including Mr. Solomon, losing the ability to commit suicide is even more haunting.

Chapter VIII: History

Depression has been with us a long time. Discussion of early description and treatment of depression throughout history and literature could fill a book; Mr. Solomon gives it pages 285-334. Of most interest is the source for the book title, *The Noonday Demon,* which comes from Cassian, who, in Psalms, describes what we define as depression as the noonday demon, melancholia, a sin that consumes the day and night. Most demons need the cover of night, but "Depression stands in full glare of the sun, unchallenged by recognition." (293).

I have used the term "demons" in a student's sentence to stimulate writing classes: "You don't know the demons in my head." That sentence has elicited some of the liveliest writings and class discussions from both teens and senior citizens. My friend, waiting for my Mr. Solomon abridgement, often tells me of the voices in her head, which she also calls "the demons." Though I understand the need for the chapter, I did not find it as essential as others.

Chapter IX: Poverty

If the previous chapter elicited minimal interest from me, this one was a "dark horse" — one I expected to be mildly interesting and turned out to be one of my top three. In it, Mr. Solomon advocates for a class to which he doesn't belong, without giving other classes or groups the same space of attention, thereby highlighting poverty's singularity. So often, we advise people to pull themselves up by their bootstraps. Solomon says the poor may "have no bootstraps and cannot pull themselves up" (336). In my own life, especially with reference to my mother, I have often asked, "What if you don't have the bootstrap gene?"

The poor require intervention, medication, and therapy. They often pass problems on to children. As a society, we could save money by treating the poor, among whom there is no depression screening. Solomon's reaction to case studies and his inclusion of people and their stories fascinate in the same way we rush toward an accident but turn our faces at the gruesome sights.

"The truth I had discovered was intolerably stranger than fiction." (360). Mr. Solomon had to rewrite a version of the chapter in a newsmagazine because editors thought that readers would not believe it. We need to empower the trained and professionals.

I liked this chapter, particularly, because Mr. Solomon states that, by helping adults with depression, we help children, who will then have a chance at a better life.

Chapter X: Politics

The topic of this chapter put me off; the writing put me on. Mr. Solomon makes sense about the attention that is necessary to devote to politics regarding depression. Politics determine treatment, by whom, where, diagnosis, and funding intervention. Definitions influence policy, which affects sufferers. Depressed people are the new invisible people. Depression is the last label in the frontier to be revealed, and coming out about it must be encouraged.

Some of us exude confidentiality to friends but continue to hear the warning about not sharing what we were told. The warning is especially reiterated when the topic is depression. There is a danger, here, of being tiresome, believing that all anyone wants to hear about is your depression. Prejudice is alive and well around this disease, too, even though notables have experienced it.

It is costly: $2,000-2,500 for the simplest depression, and three weeks of hospitalization starts at $14,000 (371). Mr. Solomon has gone to Washington as a journalist and activist and requested a hearing on suicide because we lose 31,000 people a year to it. The state with the best record for those depressed? Pennsylvania, where exemplary supportive systems exist. "Depression, like sex, retains an unquenchable aura of mystery. It is new every time." (400).

Chapter XI: Evolution

Where and how does depression fit in with the development of human beings? Though somewhat technical, I think Solomon included this chapter because, without it, his credibility would be vulnerable, and its inclusion is essential to the cause of treating depression.

Chapter XII: Hope

This is my favorite chapter. If you can only read one chapter in the book, make it this one. In these pages, you will meet Angel, whose poem I quoted earlier. Here, you will read his purpose and his bias, the need for a sense of humor, irretrievable time, the importance of love, and what you can do for depressed friends and relatives. The slogan is "blunt their isolation" (437), and I include it here because of the importance of the message and to confound any delay of action and because people need each other — now.

Notes, bibliography, and index sections end the book. I have used each of these sections to find more information, and I praise their inclusion. For his sake, I hope that the next adverse topic about which Solomon writes he has to experience vicariously. If there is any gift from his experience with depression, it goes to the reader. Solomon has made depression understandable. As an atlas, it is only one man's journey, but he speaks for many who deserve to be heard by so many more.

The Rider

Gary Bolstridge

As I drove my Chevy Blazer to work early one morning, a slight rustling sound behind me intruded on the quiet acoustic guitar music I was listening to. The sound of the stiff plastic wrap crumpling gradually grew into a continuous mashing of invasive noise. I looked in the rearview mirror and discovered that an opened package of prune cookies, kept in the car for my wife's elderly, infirm aunt, was the source of the noise. The cookies served the dual purposes of keeping the aunt occupied with chewing and keeping her... well, the obvious effect that prunes have on the digestive system.

The autumn morning was cool, but warm enough for me to have my windows down. I chalked up the movement of the cookie package to the wind blowing through the truck while I was driving. But the package continued to move as I waited at a red light. Somehow, the prune cookies were affecting the movement of their packaging. After clearing the light, I pulled over to investigate the source of the sounds in the empty parking lot of a business about to awaken for the day.

I turned in my seat to look at the spiraling container but could see only its random motions, not the source of its movement. Getting out of the truck, I opened the rear hatch and reached for the package. The movement suddenly stopped. I withdrew my hand and stood there staring, surprised. When all was quiet, the cookie package started tossing and turning again. By now, the hackles on my neck were stimulating scenarios in my mind. As I reached once more for the cookie package, out popped the head of a mouse. Our eyes locked; neither of us moved. Each of us trying to make sense out of the other's unexpected presence.

Naturally, the mouse reached a logical explanation of the situation first and immediately ran out of the package, scurrying beneath the two front seats. I was left with the dilemma of how to regain control of my vehicle without putting myself in danger. Walking over to the passenger side, I opened the door, expecting the mouse to take advantage of the opportunity to escape. No movement. I cautiously flipped the seat forward, peering behind it for signs of the intruder. There were none. I became a bit bolder and stuck my head into the vehicle, looking for him. Suddenly, on the opposite side of the truck, behind the drivers seat, his little head peeked out, large eyes focused on me, ears at full extension, his nose twitching, examining the smell of my intentions. After the initial shock of being surprised, I thought he would want to leave through his side of the truck. Willing to oblige, I rushed around the vehicle, opened the drivers' side door, and stood back. No movement. I then peered into the truck and didn't see him until his little head popped up where mine had been a moment ago, all of his senses once again directed toward me.

With both doors of the truck wide open and the seats tipped forward, any direction in which the stowaway chose to move would provide escape. I circled to his side of the truck, and he mirrored my movement, trading places to once again stare at me from my previous position. We repeated this dance a few more times before I realized the futility of the situation. I got back into the truck, closed the doors, and continued to drive to work, the music turned off so I could concentrate on the movements of my passenger and whether he posed any danger of an ambush directed toward me.

I arrived safely at work and, once again, opened the truck doors and tipped the seats forward. But there were no signs of the intruder. I left the truck fully open and went into my building to begin my day.

When I returned to the truck a half-hour later, I found everything quiet and still. I bravely, but cautiously, moved the seats forward in search of the mouse. The truck was empty! He had moved on to make a new life for himself.

But it wasn't going to be easy for him, at least at first. I lifted the once half-full package of cookies and found it completely empty. He had eaten the entire contents and was undoubtedly proceeding in his new environment at a slow pace, making, I am sure, frequent stops. I don't think he will be jumping up in any trucks for a while.

Gary Bolstridge

In a Dream

89
Dragons
Gary Bolstridge

91
from *At First You See It...*
A. Valentine Smith

95
from *The Toonijuk*
Bill Goetzinger

125
Sweet Blood
Gary Bolstridge

131
from *A Circle of Two*
A. Valentine Smith

134
Life Grows Richer Still
Ingrid Mathews

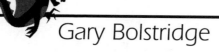

Dragons

Gary Bolstridge

A ll dragons fly. In the old days, people could see dragons — both in the sky and walking the earth. Dragons live inside of stones, exist in artworks, and sleep in caves to avoid detection. When they leave a piece of artwork, the paper or canvas that contains them disintegrates, freeing the dragons from their slumber.

In the past, many dragons were slain. The slayers' deeds were well celebrated — rationalists helping to rid the world of myth and magic. But fortunately some of the dragons survived. They have learned to make detection difficult — but not impossible. They have adopted furtive guises for this purpose. Dragons are not sneaky — they always tell the truth when confronted; they are just cautious. No sense inviting danger. For if they are detected, it hampers the business they are conducting. The person who observes them becomes fixed on the reality of the moment, defining the physical presence of the dragon. The mind is no longer receptive to suggestion.

I personally saw a dragon fly over my head one day. It was a clear day, with many clouds in the sky. The transition from summer to autumn — cool, but still dominated by warm winds. As soon as the dragon realized he was being observed (they are very sensitive, you know), he immediately began to transform into a cloud. They change like chameleons, blending in with their surroundings. Because I was looking in the right spot at the right time, he stopped his transformation mid-process and retained most of his dragon form, having only enough time to blur his general outline. It was not enough to prevent my seeing him, or at least seeing enough of him to realize that he was actually there. I briefly turned my eyes away from that spot in the sky to look at the road on which I was driving my car. This gave him enough time to complete his transformation.

Gary Bolstridge

He was now cloaked as one of those clouds, which have no discernible shape. Sort of like jazz filling the sky. You know there is a melody somewhere, but it has been disassembled and scattered with additional notes added, making the actual structure difficult to recognize. I continued driving, but my thoughts were focused on the dragon, proving the need for their concealment. My mind was no longer open to suggestion.

Evidence that dragons exist can still be found today, though it is getting more difficult to find — and it's just as well that I am speaking of it now. Our thoughts help to keep the dragons alive. Have you ever felt a warm or hot wind blow across your face, not knowing where the breeze originates? It is the dragons' breath blowing imagination and dreams into your soul — proof that dragons do exist. But dreams and imagination are getting more difficult to find today — proof of the dragons' disappearance. The more we talk of dragons and live out the inspiration of dreams and imagination that they instill in us, the longer they will remain with us.

from At First You See It...

A. Valentine Smith

"**S**he has to go."

Molly was mortified. It was bad enough that her eyes were swimming and her teeth were tightly clenched, but to have her father treat her like a preschooler when she'd just entered Junior High was awful.

"I have no idea where this exit came from, but the next one on your map is thirty miles away. Look Grace... if there's nothing down there, the worst you'd have to do is take her into the woods." Sam, her father, tried to see down the exit's path as he steered.

"Hmmm." Molly's mom frowned and stared harder at her map. Their car cleared the bushes lining the exit and ending at a small landing on the ocean. The family piled out. Sam walked up to the first person he saw. Everyone was staring out at the sea.

"Excuse me. Is there a restroom around here?" Sam asked a big-boned man in a sheriff's uniform. The uniform looked a little out of date, like maybe it was from the 50s. The sheriff did a double take.

"What are you doing here?"

"It's a bit of an emergency. Restroom?" The man pointed to a row of fiberglass-shelled temporary toilets. Holding her arms down in front of her with fists knotted tight, Molly sprinted the rest of the distance to the portable restrooms.

"Can you see the approaching boat?" the sheriff asked. He peeled off old-looking wire-rimmed sunglasses.

"Uh, no. Wait a second... yes," Sam answered. He shielded his eyes with a hand and squinted out over the ocean. A broad smile formed on the sheriff's face.

"Where's my manners. I'm Sheriff Lawless. Yeah... I know, I know. I've heard all the jokes." He extended a heavy hand, dried, cracked, and callused. Sam could feel a fat ring when he completed the shake.

"I still can't see this exit." Grace frowned as she looked down at the map. It hung like an accordion in her small hands.

A large hand mashed down on the folds.

"They never get those maps right. Never had much use for them myself." The sheriff gave them a toothy grin. "Hey where're you from? On vacation?"

"Uh... Yes. We're from Boston," Sam said.

"Oh really!" The Sheriff's grin grew larger. It became a cavern of teeth. "Live there?" He looked almost hopeful.

"Well... er... yes... and no. I just got a job up there. We're staying in a hotel while we look for somewhere to live."

"I still can't see where we are," Grace said. She tried to undo the crumpling the map had borne from the sheriff's assault.

"Housing prices out of control?" The sheriff's eyes bored straight into Sam's.

"Yea," Sam sighed. "We took this trip hoping to spot a reasonable home without too bad a commute."

"Well, why don't you take a little trip to our island. There's a house that just came to market. The previous owners are dying to sell. I'll bet you the price will be more than reasonable."

"Uh, reasonable?" Sam's face shined for the first time in weeks.

"I don't know dear. This place looks remote." Grace grabbed her husbands arm tight.

"It's an easy commute. C'mon. It won't hurt to look." The sheriff said. He began to perspire lightly. *Must have high blood pressure,* Sam thought.

"OK. Oh no. Forget it. There's no room for our car." Sam looked at the ferry. It was small and already at its four-car capacity."

"Of course there's room. Caleb!" the sheriff shouted. A balding, thin, boney man focused guarded eyes on the sheriff.

"You were just leaving Caleb, weren't you." Caleb opened his mouth into a silent "O," then closed it. His face darkened. Caleb turned without a word and headed toward a car on the ferry. A moment later, a space had opened up on the ferry's lower deck.

Molly came back, looking relieved. She saw her parents talking to a strange man. Molly had a well-developed sixth sense. Every time she ignored it, she paid a price. Right now all alarms were going off.

"I'm done Dad. Let's get going."

"Molly, we're gonna go exploring. There's a house to look at on an island."

Sam's daughter groaned. This was like the thousandth house she'd been dragged through on this so-called vacation. She looked around, her quick glance darting from face to face. A car was backing off the ferry. Nothing out of the ordinary, and yet it didn't feel right.

"Mom, Dad... let's go. Can we please?"

"Molly, I know this vacation has been something of a bust, but there might be a house for us here. You know how hard we've looked." Sam was practically salivating. Molly had seen that look before; there was no turning her dad back when he got this excited about anything. "Look Molly, I promise. We'll go straight back to Boston after visiting this island... OK?" Molly just nodded and looked at her shoes.

When they drove the car onto the ferry, Sam rolled down his window and handed the captain a credit card.

"Don't take no plastic."

"I don't have any cash." The captain shrugged and stared at Sam with unblinking eyes. He scratched his white beard and waited for them to back off his boat.

"Hold on Eustis. I'll pay for these people." The sheriff materialized out of the gloom of the lower deck and began peeling bills off a roll. The captain took the bills and signaled the first mate. He headed toward the bow.

"Thanks... uh." Sam couldn't remember. Did the sheriff give him his name?

"Lawless... Sheriff Lawless... but you can call me Manson."

"Look, we really can't take advantage of your kindness. At least let me write you a check."

"I couldn't accept. You folks look hungry. I'll take you to the best diner on the island. Buy me lunch, and we'll call it even."

Sam shrugged. "OK... thanks." A moment later, he and Grace were on the observation deck above the cars, planting themselves near the bow railing at the port side of the boat. Looking down, Sam caught sight of the man who had taken his car off the ferry. The man slammed the door shut and hurried back to the boat before it pulled completely away from the dock. He jumped hard and cleared the rapidly growing gap of water, landing on the lower deck. *Odd, I thought he just arrived.* Sam's thoughts were interrupted by a blast from the ferry's horns as it glided away from its moorings. Grace looked behind her. Molly was gone.

Standing on the farthest point of the bow, forward of the car bay, Molly steadied herself against the bright chrome railing. The wind whipped her long hair.

Do I dare? Molly looked around carefully to see if anyone was watching. No one near. Turning again to face the ocean, Molly took a deep breath and slowly raised her arms until they were parallel with her shoulders, imitating her favorite heroine from a famous ocean-liner shipwreck movie. If anyone had seen her, she'd have turned redder than her hair. The wind felt good as it flapped the sleeves of her blouse.

"Rogue wave!" shouted the first mate. His voice raised in pitch. The captain saw the wave. There was no time... no warning the passengers. He threw the wheel hard and tried to point the bow into the oncoming wave. People, drinks, and food all lurched to the right. Bags and luggage skittered across the decks, hitting people and bulkheads.

The wave caught Molly off guard. Her ribs bounced painfully off the railing. She almost fell overboard as she clawed for a hold. A wall of water, taller than the first deck, crashed over the bow.

From where she stood, welded to the upper deck railing, Grace saw her daughter disappear under a rolling sheet of water. She couldn't breath as Molly disappeared.

The wave passed. Like a rock being exposed by a retreating wave at the beach, Molly was revealed, jammed against the lower railing, gasping for air. Her previously empty hand clutched half of a broken amulet.

Her eyes were screwed shut. Searing head pain. Then she saw, like a dream, a woman and a small child. Their cloths were strange and old fashioned. The woman was doing something to the girl's hand.

from The Toonijuk

Bill Goetzinger

Northland

Squatting on the ice, hiding behind the crafted snow mound, the Toonijuk watched the black water of the narrow lead. Hearing a gurgle and seeing an outline of heat deep beneath the surface, she lowered her body behind the camouflage mound, praying her coverings, stitched from fox and seal pup, would keep her well camouflaged. If the seal saw Toonijuk darkness against the Northland white... !

But the Hunt-Spirit showed mercy this day. The Toonijuk soon heard a paddling, then the scramble of claws on the shelf as the seal hauled out.

There was a sliding. Breathing.

She tensed, hand tightening on her walrus tusk. The seal moved closer...

...and the Toonijuk sprang. Hopping to her feet. Leaping over the snow-mound.

Karunk! The round eyes of a large gray-black male looked straight at her. As she rushed him, the seal whirled and slid quickly back toward the water.

The Toonijuk dove, belly-landing on the ice. Gliding down beside the seal. She extended her left arm, wrapping it around his neck.

He barked. Lashed out with his flippers. Digging her toes into the snow and ice, she dropped the tusk and forced herself to her knees. Her free hand balled, and she pounded the base of the seal's head.

The blow left him dazed, but still thrashing. Taking hold of a forelimb, she rolled him on his back. He warbled in protest as she straddled the belly, plucking the tusk from the snow. With both hands she raised the clan totem high above her head and plunged it into the throat. The seal twitched once then lay still.

Exhausted, the Toonijuk fell on the carcass. Enjoying the dying warmth, she rested, regaining her strength.

Finally she stood, study-viewed her hunt-kill, and yelped in surprise. A very big seal! Head bigger than this Toonijuk! Would that her father had seen such a kill!

She would eat what she could. Cache the rest. From this excellent skin she would craft new coverings, footwear, and perhaps a blanket. And from the bones, she would...

The Toonijuk paused. Certain she'd heard the barest squeak of crunching snow.

She listened carefully. Scanned the ice. The sound had come from a nearby cluster of windswept ridges. She'd negotiated them herself in order to reach this smoother plane. They had hidden her well enough. Could hide something bigger.

She removed the tusk from the seal's throat.

There was another sound, a footfall.

She pinpointed the noise-source. There, behind a hummock.

Only a walk away!

The Toonijuk clenched the tusk.

From behind the hummock emerged a four-legged form, huge and white.

Toonijuk's heart beat rapidly. She shook.

For this was her enemy.

The Bear!

He strode rapidly toward her, moving like flowing water over the rough, broken ice. Crossing over onto the plane, he increased his speed, coming at the Toonijuk with hare-fast bounds.

A voice of elder-wisdom screamed for her to run. Told her that the bear only wished to steal the kill and would leave her alone. But she also remembered the long time without food. Abandon this hunt-kill, and she might never find another. Might very well starve here on the Frozen Sea.

No. The kill belonged to this Toonijuk. She stood her ground.

The bear continued his charge. He was young, lean, with insolent eyes. He came closer and closer, and the Toonijuk did her best not to tremble as she gazed at those powerful limbs and mighty paws. The bear ran faster. Only a pace away...

Brandishing her weapon, the Toonijuk bellowed. Bellowed with all her might, at the top of her lungs, while waving the tusk.

Looking surprised, the bear skidded to a halt, splattering snow.

The Toonijuk made a jabbing motion with the tusk. Placed a foot on the seal's head, and thunked her chest, saying, "This my kill! Toonijuk belong! My enemy leave!"

But her enemy didn't leave. He grunted, pawed the ice, and swayed his weasel-slender head, taking in this Quoo Toonijuk who dared challenge him over kill-claim.

Then he moved a step forward. The Toonijuk repeated her display, waving the tusk and bellowing even more loudly.

The bear roared. Revealed fangs as big as spear-points. The Toonijuk quaked.

Smelling fear, the bear moved in.

Even on all legs his nose stood level with her chest. She backed from her kill.

But when the bear reached the carcass, he stepped over it, and kept walking.

And the Toonijuk understood.

Understood the bear, like this Toonijuk, was a wanderer, who, also like her, had gone a long while without food. The fit of his thin coat over rangy muscles showed her how hungry he must be. Hungry enough not to settle for one meal when he might have two.

The bear pressed forward. She backed away, her weapon feeling light and useless. The bear seemed to grin at her cowardice.

No, she thought, firming tusk-grip. Be no frightened Mitt! Remember elder-lessons.

The bear rushed her. Rose to his hind legs, standing twice her height. Swept his left paw back.

While the Toonijuk remembered the first lesson...

...and darted straight at the bear. Straight in the path of the kill-strike.

As the paw and claws came within a midge of her face, the Toonijuk ducked, hair ruffling as near-death swept over her head. Then...

...she dove to the bear's left, under the pit of his arm.

Heard a *whoosh* as the strike completed its arc across the width of the bear's chest, no Toonijuk halting the sweep. Down he went to all fours, bumping the Toonijuk as she zagged by, knocking the tusk from her hand.

Spat!

The Toonijuk ran.

Ran for the cluster of ridges, where she hoped she might evade pursuit. But as she built up speed, she heard the scrape of ice as the bear pivoted, followed by the pounding of sprinting feet. Hot breath licked her nape, and a violent force seized her by the outer-coverings, jerking the Toonijuk in place before yanking her backwards.

She bent her toes down, spiking her nails into the ice. Chips flew as she slowed and slowed until she stopped entirely. For a horrible moment bear-strength tested Toonijuk-ice-hold in a vicious tug-game, then...

...*rip,* and she tumbled forward, rolling with the fall and ending up on her knees, facing her opponent.

He held a stitch of fox-coverings in his right paw. With a frustrated growl, he cast them aside and lunged at the Toonijuk.

She scrambled to her feet. By the time she got to them, he was already upon her. Rearing, clamping front paws on her shoulders.

She staggered under the weight, knees buckling, shrieking as claws poked through her coverings and sank into her flesh.

She looked up at the sharp-toothed maw, opening wide. As the head dipped down, she thrust her hands up, catching the bear's chin...

And pushed, pushed!

Arms and legs trembled. She screamed as claws shredded her back. Yelled "Getoff!" at her foe. But, chortling, he kept exerting his awesome mass.

They spun, round and round. The bear whipped out his tongue, dripping saliva on her face.

WhattodoWhattodo? Use whatever means you can, the Elders had taught. Nails, feet, and?

Yes!

The left paw touched her chin. Taking her sight from those jaws, she turned her head, opened her mouth wide, and bit.

The bear at first gave no notice, but she bit down harder and harder until she tasted blubber and blood.

Breaking free of her hold, the bear snapped his head back and howled. Released her. She stumbled away and collapsed. The bear rolled on the ice, whining as he staunched the wound with snow.

Blood darkened the blue-white under her. Back ached. She sat up, catching her breath.

Only a pace away was the lead. Waters would have frozen some by now, but not completely. There was a hope she might try...

...if she was youth-fool enough to dare.

The bear growled at her. An almost friendly growl, wound quickly forgotten. Navra! He was enjoying himself!

He rose to fours. The Toonijuk started to crawl on hands and knees toward the lead.

And again the bear lunged.

She crawled faster, faster, but no good; the bear caught up.

So she flipped on her back. Met his black eyes...

...and kicked, sending her foot into his nose. Anger in the strike because the seal, she knew, was lost. She heard a *crunch!*

And the bear mewed and placed paws on snout. The Toonijuk slapped her forearm, extended index and middle finger at him...

Eat Toonijuk spatt, O' enemy!

...and, lowering her membranes, taking a deep influx of breath, she crawled then slid into the open water.

A cold shock as she cut through the crystallizing surface and submerged. She paddled, kicked, and descended past the thick of the ice ledge. Heard above a splash. The paw or head, maybe, but not the whole bear. Be reluctant to get salt water in a fresh wound. Endure stinging pain as the Toonijuk did now, making her want to scream and scream in agony! The only feeling she might have for awhile.

For though the bear might not plunge in after her, the Demon of the Northland was ever the patient hunter and would stalk along the lead, waiting for the Toonijuk to emerge for precious air.

So she wouldn't.

The loose fox-coverings trapped bubbles, slowing her, putting her at risk. So, as she reached the bottom of the ledge, she stripped down to the seal coverings, allowing the old outer coat to drift away with the current.

All sensation had left her fingers and toes and soon would leave most of her body. Her head, though, felt as if it were swelling, and her chest caved inwards. She became acutely aware of her heart, beating less and less until it barely seemed to beat at all. The Toonijuk stopped swimming, allowing the frigid water to suck her down. When she had sunk well below the ledge, she began to kick and paddle again, swimming directly under the floes. With this part of the Frozen Sea as thick as a whale was long, all light soon vanished.

But even without sight, she continued to sense the ice, and kept well below it, careful to make as little noise as possible. The bear might be trying to stalk from above.

Her body became almost fully numb, and even the sting of her injuries lessened. The Toonijuk realized the full madness of what she was doing. Yes, she had taken to the water before and had swum for great lengths under the floes. She was an excellent swimmer, her father had always said. But never had she — or any Toonijuk — ever swum underwater in the winter, beneath such a vast expanse of ice!

For Toonijuk were, like all Northland dwellers, not fish; they needed to come to the surface for life-air. And Toonijuk were not the Seal or the Walrus, or even the Bear. They might only stay underwater but a few moments...

...or stay there forever!

She swam as fast as she could, but moving her right arm brought pain to her back. What had the bear done? No way to see. The Walrus had gouged her once, but this hurt even worse. Hopefully, the Healer-Spirit might soon mend it.

She scanned continuously for light. But the passing waters remained as black as Lok, and the Toonijuk half-expected to see Navra herself, questing for a spirit to devour.

But while she didn't see the Mistress of the Underland, the Toonijuk did see ghost-light of fish and other waterlife. Thankfully, she did not see the brighter flashes of the Walrus or the Orca, which at least gave off light, unlike the Bear.

She swam on, trying to remember the lay of the surface ice, trying to remember everything she had seen before reaching the lead where she had caught the seal. But the ice, even a Quoo Toonijuk knew, was like one alive. Shifting, moving, changing. What she had seen a twilight ago might be long gone.

The ice now turned a shade blue. Thinning, but still too thick to break and stretching on endlessly.

She swam and swam. Tiring, chest hurting, wanting to breath. Too long under. She grew lightheaded. Wondered if this be the work of the Gods, seeking to punish her — first through the bear, and now by drowning under the Frozen Sea.

Punish this Toonijuk for her great sin.

And should I not accept such punishment and at least see family and Clan-Mates in the Sky-Ground?

But as she swam a length more, she saw something that made her vanish such mad thoughts. Made her heart soar.

Ahead, a great stretch of ice, light blue from below, as blue as the sky on a bright summer day. A newly frozen lead she had crossed a stretch of time ago. So new it had sagged beneath her weight. Firmer now, no doubt, but still thin enough to break.

Maybe...

Her injured, exhausted shell took forever to reach the new-ice cutting across the older floes. Chest hurt more; spots danced in her vision. Needed air now, but once she was under the frozen lead, she dove a few strokes down then back-swam. A weak current took her, allowing her to rest some as she study-gazed for the thinnest ice.

Sighting a particularly light portion, she kicked upwards and swam to it.

The ice was smooth, translucent, and yet strong. With her more powerful left arm, she struck it.

Nothing. Didn't even bend.

Struck with both arms. Still nothing.

Kicked. Nothing. Struck and kicked. Nothing. Nothing.

Nothing!

No good! The Walrus couldn't break through, let alone a Toonijuk. And no other thin ice in sight! Indeed, nothing in sight, as everything, even the blue above, grew darker and darker and...

...?

And she saw other Toonijuk around her. Not treading water, but standing, as if on the land-ground. Not mad with this Toonijuk as she felt they should be, but speaking. Her father, offering a blessing of the Protector-Spirit. And the ancient Shaman, telling her she must break through the ice. Break through to start her journey-way.

????

Lightness returned, and she saw no Toonijuk. Only the dark water and frozen lead, now many strokes above.

!!!!

She had fallen asleep! Was sinking! Had been elder-warned that spending too long underwater might cause loss of awareness. Next time, she might never wake. But she couldn't get to surface! She couldn't?

No! Must drive fear from mind! Must be calm.

Relax-self, her father would say. *Study-view the ice.*

She did. Concentrated on the differing patterns of light, looking for? Yes!

There, only a short swim away. A round patch, a half-shade lighter than its surroundings. Maybe worn down by current or broken through by the Walrus — mattered nothing to this Toonijuk.

She kicked furiously over and struck the ice with both hands. Again, it didn't break but did stretch like the fish-skin of a game-pouch. A little more pressure!

She dropped. Focused...

Even as her chest hammered and her vision started to dim.

Ayaa!

Using every last bit of strength, she swam.

Straight up. Arms out. Palms flat.

Straight into weak ice.

It stretched. Stretched...

...and...

Smash!

...shattered!

Shards fell on her head, others slid across smooth glaze. The Toonijuk heard a *huh-uh! huh-uh! huh-uh! huh-uh!* and realized it was herself, taking in over-needed air.

Grabbing the edges of the hole, she hauled out onto the firmer new-ice. Her face and body tingled. Grew warm. Chest expanded. Heart beat faster. The agonizing pain in her back returned. She shook and shook her head, ridding it of water, and raised her membranes.

Then she belly-crawled farther — tentatively. When she felt sure the ice would support her, she rose to hands and knees and shook off the water before it froze.

Up on her feet now, skating across the frozen lead until she reached the denser pack ice. Once there, she stripped off her seal-skin coverings and plunged in snow, rolling and rolling to blot off every last trace of water.

When done, she hopped up, looking, listening, and smelling for enemy.

But of the Bear there was no sign. She was safe.

Safe and in-shell. But just barely. For the first time she reached back to check her wounds. Digging a finger into deep gashes. She dabbed them with snow, praying the Healer-Spirit might work her magic. Bad cuts; had those claws been any deeper...

She shook, thinking not just of the bear but the time under the ice.

Then anger took hold. She stomped. Raven-thief bear! No doubt now enjoying her hard-won kill.

Still, she thought with a grin, he also bore Toonijuk-inflicted injury and would not soon forget his combat with this one!

Fighting the boar Bear and swimming beneath the Frozen Sea in winter. Feats to tell the Clan! Feats to impress even the Great-Lord and Monster-Slayer Grundun. Even this Toonijuk's big-head brother might have been amazed.

She smiled, thinking these things. Thinking of Clan...

...and thinking these things, began to cry.

Could not tell the Clan of her feats, she knew, because her mother and father and brothers and the ancient Shaman and other Clan-Mates were all gone.

All dead.

Killed by an enemy even worse than the Bear of the Snows.

And now this most unworthy daughter had even lost the tusk, totem of the Walrus Clan.

She kept crying even as she crafted a den from bits of rubble ice. Even as she slept within, sleeping as the lone Toonijuk must, with an eye and ear always keeping watch. With a rumbling stomach and a thumb in this one's mouth, in a way not done since a Mitt.

When the Toonijuk awoke she pushed aside the ice-plug and crawled from the cramped den. She stretched, glanced carefully about for enemy or prey, then checked her wounds. The bleeding, she discovered, had stopped, and even the gashes felt smaller in size. Soon they would close entirely. The Healer-Spirit worked great magic and worked it quickly. No other Northland dwellers were as blessed. Why should this be, she had one time asked the Shaman. But even he did not know.

The Toonijuk now turned her mind to an important decision: should she continue northward, on the Frozen Sea? Or make the long walk back south and return to the land?

She missed the land. Missed the rocky shores and high cliffs and towering glaciers. Missed the Great Cave, just as she missed the Toonijuk who once dwelled there. She could at least sleep in the cave, maybe long-sleep. Better than in an ice-den!

The land called her home. So what reasons did this one have for staying on the Frozen Sea? She'd hoped to find large game, but without the white coverings for camouflage, the Toonijuk would have trouble stalking even the dumbest seal. Needed a good, long spear, but now this youth-fool did not even have the tusk or cutting tool!

So, the Toonijuk asked herself: did any other reasons exist for staying on the Frozen Sea, with its treacherous ice and the prowling Bear?

She meditated deeply for an answer but could only think of one.

Something that had started her on this long walkabout. An idea that had first made her hope-filled. But after much walking and walking, and seeing nothing but ice and snow and snow and ice, this one's hope had faded as light from winter's sky, making her sadder and sadder.

The hope was that she might find, out here on the floes, other Toonijuk Clans. Like the Orca Clan, who had lived southways, along the coast, and the Loon Clan, who had made their home near the ice fields. This Toonijuk had journeyed to both their grounds, hoping to gain acceptance, but had found not so much as a sign of Toonijuk. Had these worthy people also been slaughtered like hers? Or had they fled across the ice? Fled from the most terrible of enemies?

But if Toonijuk were out here, then why has she found neither scat nor scent? Might find such things, she knew, after much travel. But without food, how could a lone Quoo hope to survive long on the Frozen Sea?

Karunk! What should this one do? She needed the wisdom of a Ka-Tornqua and the advice of the Elder-Council to make such a decision.

But before she made it, before she went either north or south, there was something she needed to do. For herself...

...and the Clan.

By following her old scent and the lay of ice, she soon arrived at the narrow lead where she had encountered the bear, who had since departed, of course. A wanderer seldom stayed in one place; by now he was probably many walks away.

Gone too was the seal carcass, a bloody spot where it had lain. But what of the...

The Toonijuk went over to the camouflage-mound, seeing what she had feared. The bear had discovered her walrus-skin pouch, and, either out of hunger or rage had shredded and partially devoured it. Its contents, at least, were intact, if scattered. Right away she found her necklace, and wondered if the bear had noticed it was made from the claws of one of his fellows. She put it on then hunted about until she found the cut of narwhal tusk she used for a fish-spear, and the wristlet woven from musk ox hair, adorned with a piece of ivory carved in the image of Gundrun, the Wayfarer, without which the Guide-Spirits wouldn't help her.

But search as she did, the Toonijuk couldn't find the one object she most desperately sought.

She stomped in frustration. Cried. Chewed her thumb.

Felt a tingle on her neck.

And, for no reason that could be thought, she suddenly followed a straight line some paces to a body-deep crevasse. There, at the bottom, its black squiggly markings clearly visible, lay the tusk.

Retrieving it, the Toonijuk thanked the Spirits.

However, though she looked and looked, she was unable to find the cutting-tool! Remembering she had left it on the carcass, the Toonijuk reckoned it had fallen into the lead and now was deep in the waters, forever beyond reach.

Karunk! she thought. How was she supposed to cut meat? Assuming, that was, she even found meat to cut?

The loss of the cutting-tool eased her big decision. Nevertheless, she gazed northward at white and gray and more unbroken white. Stretching for walks and walks.

A wind kicked up, brushing a spectral flurry of snow across the icescape. It seemed to speak her True Name, beckoning for her to continue the trek across the Frozen Sea.

But her Spirit-of-Shell cried for land's return. And hadn't she been elder-taught to listen to this voice always? So, tusk in one hand, fish-spear in the other, the last surviving daughter of the Walrus Clan headed south. Headed home.

As north, so south.

Journey-way with life-threat every few steps. Many times did the Toonijuk dodge the Bear, though none, praise Gundrun, came as close as the hunt-kill Raven-thief had!

The greatest danger, of course, as she had been taught and now experience-learned, was the ice itself, always moving and cracking open. She kept her eyes to the stars to keep her direction-sense and often stopped, waiting for wide leads to freeze over. Normally, she might try to swim across, but without the pouch, her hands were too full, and, what's more, she was too tired. Every time she lay down, she found herself not wanting to get back up.

Once, during such a resting, she nearly got caught in an ice-breaking. Only through sense of water and vibration did she manage to flee the ice before it cracked and erupted beneath her feet. And there were squalls, with winds strong enough to knock even the largest Elder down. But the squalls never caught this one off guard. Ears pricked before she even saw one approach. Toonijuk danger-sense was good.

But as she sheltered in an ice-den from yet another storm, she thought upon this danger-sense. Where was it on that day? The day she could not forget. A warm sunny day with the smell of fish in the air. A smell that grew stronger as her people, bringing skins and narwhal tusks, had come down from the hills, this one small enough to still ride her father's back. No fear or caution had they shown, no weapons had they carried, no danger had any felt...

Except for her.

It had been as though a chill breeze had run up her back. And everything had suddenly seemed wrong. Looking down at the square-edged "wood" dwellings on the rocky shore below, this Toonijuk had not seen what should have been seen. The ones who lived there. Playing, working. There was only a weird stillness. A lifelessness. All wrong.

The Shaman had told her to never ignore such feelings, and she had promptly told her father and the others, getting them to stop. But her father had thought she might have been ill-at-ease because, a few days before, the Shaman had dreamed of the Raven chasing the Wolf, a bad omen. The ancient one had promptly traveled to the Sacred Place high in the ice fields to speak with the Ghosts. Learn the vision-meaning. He had not yet returned, but this was nothing unusual as a Dream-Quest might take well over a season.

So when someone had finally emerged from a dwelling of "wood," walking over to the round Naked-make storage-holds where the fish was kept and waving to the Toonijuk on the hill above, her father had ruffled this ones hair, saying, "See, our sweet-pearl. Show no fear-concern. We soon have fine fish for trade!"

And, feeling a youth-fool, she had gone with the others down the hillside, the one by the storage-holds waving them closer and closer. Not until they were almost there had she seen that he was a stranger, with a scarred face and missing teeth. That much she had seen before he ran from the fish.

This one remembered the sounds that followed.

A *crack!*, like the breaking of ice, only louder and sharper. A red stain had appeared on her brother's chest as he fell. Then another *crack!* and the same had happened to her uncle. Then more *crack!*, *crack!*, *crack!*, followed by screaming and screaming and dying and running, mother shouting her name...

The Toonijuk huddled tight in the ice den, while snow piled at its mouth and buried her toes. She tried to think of happier moments, like the Clan gatherings or her time hunting with the Tornqua, but memory of that day was like a nightmare from which she couldn't awake. And in her mind-eye, she also saw the Shaman, lying as she'd found him, at the foot of a glacier, his Spirit long departed from shell, which had blackish wounds in chest and head. Wounds made by what had killed the others. What this one knew as death-spears, which killed without touching, by Naked-magic.

They had stripped the Shaman of coverings and totems, and judging from the tracks she had seen, chased him far. But the Shaman had led his pursuers uphill, far away from the Clan Grounds. This Toonijuk did not understand why, at first, because the Shaman would have been safe among Tornqua. But when she had later thought about it, she realized the Shaman had made a vain attempt to lead the killers from the grounds, just as the Jaeger lures the Fox from her nest.

And when the Toonijuk realized this, she had bit her hand and scratched her face and then run, run, until she was in the farthest chamber of the Great Cave, where she had sat huddled for days and days and days.

Just as she sat huddled now, humming, gently rocking, waiting for the storm to pass, trying to remember the way her mother and father and brothers and the old Shaman and all her other Clan-Mates had looked in life, but seeing in the flurries only blood, death...

...and monsters.

The trek southward seemed to be lasting longer than the walk north had, and the Toonijuk began to think she had lost her bearings. But she was traveling as elder-taught, by keeping the star-image of Gundrun in sight at all times, the star marking the tip of his club always to her right. Seemed the hump of the land should soon appear on the south-horizon.

Her hunger had flared, and so did her frustration after many a seal-stalking failed to end in a kill. She grew tired easily and became dizzy frequently. Many times did she stop to rest and rub feet, made sore by walking over rubble and needle ice. Sometimes, when facing difficult weather or ice, it was all she could do to walk a few paces. The urge to lie down and sleep and sleep grew increasingly inviting.

Good things happened, though. The Healer-Spirit sealed her wounds, ridding the Toonijuk of all pain. And the twilight returned, the sky changing from black to violet, meaning the sun was coming, and with it, the warm season! The thought made her happy for during the summer there was fishing and bird-snaring and games and the Ritual of the Walrus, down on the shore, and the Gathering of Clan.

But then the Toonijuk remembered that none of these things would ever be again, and the darkness returned to her Spirit. So she thought only of the journey, each step of which now required her full attention and effort anyway.

After wearing herself out by crossing a tricky mat of shifting floes, the Quoo snow-walker stopped to rest in the shadow of an embedded ice-island a walk away. It was as wide as some of the small islands off the coast of the land, and its steep ridges rose to nearly the height of the rock wall overlooking her Clan Grounds. It offered plenty of room for game to hide. The Toonijuk was thinking she might explore it when a breeze delivered an odor to her nose. A fishy odor. She followed it.

It led her some paces to a large, deep hole. And sure enough, beside the hole was a fish. A big gray fish. The Shark! Half-eaten up to the head, but still with plenty of flesh left for this one, and while it was bitter, it was still flesh. She pounced on the carcass, using her nails, teeth, and the walrus tusk, nails, and teeth to cut off a few strips, which she greedily devoured.

She finished with a loud belch and went back to cutting up more shark. Whose kill was this? she wondered. For the Shark lived deep in the waters, and even the Bear would have trouble...

She sniffed hard, now detecting odors that had been masked by shark, and crept to the slushy hole. Such a big hole, in thick ice. Too big to have been made by the Bear or anyone else, except...

She studied the snow around the hole, seeing what she had been too careless to see before.

Paw prints.

Not the Wolf. The Clan-Friend never wandered so far onto the Frozen Sea. Only one could have made these prints, and with them, she was sure to find...

Yes.

Farther from the hole was another set of prints. They were shaped much like Toonijuk footprints or the Bear's hind paw, only smaller, with no toe or claw marks. And on their insides were many tiny holes that no Northland dweller would ever leave behind.

Here also was another scent. A little sweeter than ermine musk. Salty. When the Toonijuk smelled this, she shrieked. Drew back.

Trembling, her heart stopping, she heard a *squish, squish.*

Loud footfalls on the ice. Too loud for the Bear.

She looked to the ice-island and saw a figure standing near its rim. On two legs, like a Toonijuk, but shorter. Slighter. Wearing coverings as red as blood.

It was the Naked. Killer of her family and Clan.

It stood there, looking at the Toonijuk, and the Toonijuk stood there, unmoving except for the shaking of hands and knees. Hearing the slow *thump, thump* of her heart and the whimpering of the frightened Mitt.

The Naked removed a small object from its shoulder, putting it to its face. The Toonijuk recognized this thing, a magic-piece used for sighting. The Naked continued to stare at her, its shell flashing with excitement.

And in the Toonijuk's head her people screamed and fell and died while the Naked came out from behind rocks.

Then a voice, sounding like father's, yelled, "Run!"

So the Toonijuk snatched the tusk from where it lay and ran. Once-weak legs carried her falcon-swift over the ice, bounding ridges. When she looked back, she saw the Naked running toward the ice-island, holding another object against its mouth. It moved awkwardly, stumbling to knees, giving the Toonijuk time to escape.

She realized that in her haste she had left the fish-spear behind but dared not return for it. For this Naked might be fetching a death-spear (!), which could take life over a great distance. And the Naked was never solitary. Where there was one there would be others.

She hurdled a crack and raced another few walks, finally seeking cover and her breath behind a snow bank. When she again looked back, the Naked was gone.

The Toonijuk moved swiftly thereafter, with an eye always looking behind her, doing everything elder-taught to pursuit-evade: back-walking, water-crossing, looping. She thanked the Spirits for winds that erased her prints. After a time, she felt a little safer for she saw or sensed no Naked in pursuit. But this was not reason to lower guard-sense, she knew, for though the Naked possessed not Toonijuk strength, speed, or tracking-sense, they used a powerful magic! Magic that allowed them to kill without touching and move floats without paddling. They could even move ice-sleds without the strange Naked-wolf to pull them. This one had seen such an ice-sled once. It had made a noise like the growl of the Bear.

She had also heard tell of the giant, stiff-winged birds that carried the Naked in their bellies. The Shaman himself had seen them land on the ice, and he had spoken about it with the Ka-Tornqua in the Council Chamber, while this one had pressed herself against the entrance, listening in as she shouldn't have been. She'd heard the Shaman urge caution-sense against those commanding such demons. And he had reminded the Ka-Tornqua of the once-conflict between the Naked and the People, a conflict that had ended with the Toonijuk being driven to the Northland.

But the Ka-Tornqua had said to the Shaman, "This Toonijuk gives full ear to the words spoken by the most elder-wise and revered among the Walrus Clan, but the conflict of which you speak did happen in the many ages before you and I had breathed our first air. Such ill-differences be long forgotten now, and the Naked who share our land have since become as a Clan-friend to the People. We need show no fear of them."

Hearing sense in the great Ka-Tornqua's words, this daughter had agreed, and long thought, until that day when the Toonijuk had come down from the hills for fish-for-trade. When Clan-friendship had shown itself a Raven-deceit!

She wondered if the Naked had wandered the Frozen Sea searching for the last of the Walrus Clan. It occurred to her that the enemy might also be waiting for her on the land. But she would hide in the Great Cave, whose location no Naked knew. Hide, hide, in the grounds of her people. The Naked would never find her.

The quick pace grew wearying. When the Toonijuk was absolutely sure no Naked came in pursuit, she denned for a short sleep. And when she awoke she saw the sun peaking over the south-horizon.

Day's return she would most times welcome. But the sun was as a friend to the Naked, who saw better in its light. The sun, too, brought warmth to the Northland, receding the ice. Not having the strength or will for a long swim, the Toonijuk knew she must reach the land quickly. But she still had walks and walks to go, leads to cross, the Bear to dodge.

And so the Toonijuk traveled on, while the sun rose higher and higher, until she had to lower membranes to protect her eyes from the white-glare. She crossed a vast plane then hunted alongside a perilous crevasse for an ice-bridge. After finding one, she carefully stepped across like the stealthy Fox and met her next obstacle: a steep ridge. She climbed, climbed, the effort robbing her of strength, and when she reached the top, she sat, rested, blotted sweat from her forehead and looked to see...

Distant black humps on the white.

The land!

The Toonijuk whooped in delight, skated down the other side of the ridge, and moving at a slow run, headed home.

After some time, she began to make out blue-gray cliffs and snowy plateaus. Couldn't yet see the fiord leading to the Walrus Clan Ground and the Great Cave, but it would be there. Some things never went away.

The Toonijuk faltered, asking herself what joy was in a home-return with no family or Clan to return to?

But then she heard, somewhere in the distance, a *huff!* The Walrus, breaking for air. A good omen for one of her Clan. Spirit-lifted, the Toonijuk continued on, the land appearing close enough to touch but still many walks away.

She heard a low rumble.

The ice? She checked about for cracking but saw nothing. Coming from the land, perhaps? An avalanche?

But the rumble continued to grow louder. To the Toonijuk's ears, it sounded much like the stampede of the Musk Ox. But they didn't venture on the ice. And besides, as she listened better, it seemed the rumble came from...

...the air?

She stopped. Looked about, pinpointing the sound-source until she saw, to the west, by a craggy bluff...

...a bird?

Flying her way.

Strange bird, black and large, flying not quite right. Growing larger as it approached.

The Toonijuk remained in place, fascinated, for she soon saw that this was an odd bird indeed, with wings placed far on its back, as were a mosquito's. And like that crit's, these wings beat so fast they were a blur. But no crit grew so big, the Toonijuk knew. So what might this be?

It veered leftways, giving her a better look. She saw now its shape, a head connected to a thin tail, this also with a smaller set of beating wings. The creature's four legs were as slender stems, each pair attached to only a single giant foot!

No Northland dweller be like this! The Toonijuk understood she was looking at a monster!

An orca-big monster that now turned, dipped its head downward, and flew straight at the Toonijuk.

She ran back the way she had come, hearing the *whirrrrr* of those terrible beating wings, then feeling a gust tease her hair as the monster flew right overhead. The Toonijuk made a sudden halt and switched direction, sprinting diagonally at a sharp angle. The Hare, she knew, often did such things to evade the Owl, and surely a sky-dweller this large could not quickly turn, giving her a moment to look for open water.

But she saw no cracks or leads, while she did see, from the corner of right eye, the winged demon, zooming by. It passed the Toonijuk, flew a short distance ahead, stopped, and, with the speed and flight-skill of the Falcon, turned completely around, hovering above her path, its wings not beating, she could now see, but spinning, round and round.

The Toonijuk screamed. Screamed for other Toonijuk. For the Spirits. But none came to help as the monster swooped down.

She started to run the opposite way, but as the *whirrrrr* filled her ears and spinning wings turned the air white with snow, she knew she could not outrun the monster. That her only hope was to scare it into retreat.

Facing the beast, she was surprised to find it had not completed its swoop, but instead hovered a short length above her. She brandished the tusk, bellowing, yelling *"Keepfrom! Keepfrom!"* But that black, eyeless face showed no fear nor any feeling or Spirit. Its skin looked as hard as a glacier wall. With the sun out, the Toonijuk couldn't see a shell's light, but she somehow knew whirling-wing, like Navra, had none to shine.

She bellowed again, reached down, and grabbed a handful of snow, packing it into a ball and flinging it upwards. The ball exploded on the belly, but did no harm, and instead of retreating, the monster descended. An opening appeared on its side, and from it emerged the Naked, holding and aiming a death-spear.

Shrieking, the Toonijuk started to run.

There was a *crack!*

And a sharp pain where the bear-wounds had recently healed. She kept running until it seemed she must have been crossing new ice as she suddenly wobbled and bobbed.

Dizzy too, and sleepy, but she needed to run, run. She took another few steps, feeble steps, and saw blood drops on the snow. Slowing, she touched her back and felt warm wetness and something stuck in her flesh.

Her feet hit a bump, and she fell, the walrus tusk sliding far from her grasp. But though the world raced around her and the strength fled her body, she managed to get to her feet, even as she heard another,

Crack!

And a sharpness pierced her throat. She pawed at her neck, facing the monster, which still hovered in place. Saw two, then one, then two again. The Naked with a death-spear hanging on its side.

The Toonijuk pulled from her neck what looked like a thin spearhead. Casting it aside, she heard a roaring scream that echoed across the Frozen Sea until it must have reached the land. A sound filled with rage and hate.

A sound made by her.

The ice slid from beneath her feet. The world rose and turned upside down. Falling, she saw once again the land — so close — and then there was whiteness, followed by black.

Touching.

Moving.

Floating, as she did in the summer, on her back, in the ice-clear waters of the fiord, watching gull and cormorant flying overhead.

A quick pain in the arm, then happiness, dreaming of when father took her hunting, and they sat together on a cliff, watching the dance of the Whale.

And another dream, of being in a moss-green den. Hearing guttural noises. Seeing shadowy forms that quickly disappeared. Something heavy on arms and legs.

And then a voice.

It said,

"Pearl."

And the Toonijuk opened her eyes and knew she had reached the Sky-Grounds for here was the Shaman, sitting cross-legged beside her in his chamber in the Great Cave, a fire between them. He wore his bear-skin robes and the stone walrus-mask. The sight made her happy for she knew mother and father and the others would be here as well.

"No, daughter," said the Shaman, shaking his head. "Your time be not yet to join us. But the Ghosts do speak of you, and now this old one knows what he did not know before. Why he did not earlier see, cannot be properly said. My apologies for not realizing, daughter, and for not being with you as a Shaman should."

"What?" she started to ask, for these words made no sense, but her throat was dry, voice was gone, and she spoke no more.

"There be a hope yet," said the Shaman, "if you but seek out the one, of whom I have seen a vision, here in the Ghost-land. Not as I would have chosen, but matters of the solid world be beyond a Spirit's power to control."

He rose, not stiffly as an old one, but as spryly as a young Tornqua, his Totem-staff in hand. The mask faded, revealing a face with fewer wrinkles and lines than she remembered, but still with the same silver mane and dark blue eyes. He reached over the fire for her, saying, "Beseech you, sweet pearl. Seek the one. Seek for yourself. Seek for the People."

What did he mean? Were the Toonijuk still alive? She wanted to ask, but speech would not come. She reached out, too, over the fire for the Shaman's hand. He said, "Spirits guide you, daughter."

And as their palms and fingers met, he became as a reflection on clear waters, and then was a shadowy bird like the Raven, flying away. She lost her balance, toppling from her perch into the fire. Blinding light filled her eyes...

...and she again opened them. Sticky, gummy eyes. Opened them to...

...where?

Somewhere hot. Hot, dark, with clover-soft ground, for that's what her back and head rested on. She felt sweaty, her throat and mouth so dry. There was, somewhere, a steady *beep... beep... beep.* A bird of some unknown kind.

And she was tired, groggy, and...

...awake. Alive! Spirit still in shell!

But where was she?

The Toonijuk blinked her membranes, clearing her eyes, allowing them to grow accustomed to the darkness, and soon saw white above. A white ceiling. She turned her head weakly about, seeing walls just as white. She understood she must be in a chamber or dwelling of sorts, but its structure seemed neither rock nor bone. Must be some light about for her to see at all. She glanced back and saw it, seeping through a column of thin lines on the wall, the weave-like texture of this section appearing different from the rest.

Where be I?

She dimly remembered the whirling-wing demon bird, the Naked emerging from within, hitting this one with his death-spear. And she had been hit. She remembered pain, blood, falling. So why was she not in the Sky-Grounds, among the other Toonijuk?

And why should she feel so hot when, last she knew, she was still on the ice, winter not yet at an end.

She raised her head, raised it from what she saw was a kind of rest, but not made from fox as a rest should be. On her body was a layer of sleep-coverings. White and dark brown, with a terrible, musty odor, smelling of neither caribou nor seal or any being that lived.

Other smells here, too. Bitter smells, like whale spat. Stung the nose. *Beep! Beep! Beep!* The bird chirped quicker. Awful sounding bird! Song flat, with no music. No Northland bird, not even the Raven, made such ungainly noise.

Where was this Toonijuk?!

No answers would come if she stayed on her back, so the Toonijuk began to rise. But as she tried, she found her arms stuck by her sides, something pressed against the wrists, as well as her belly. Couldn't get up!

Beep! Beep! Beep! Beep!

She relaxed a moment. The bird slowed its chirping. The Toonijuk then curled back her left forearm, straining against her unseen bond. Straining until...

Snap!

A brown strap flew out from beneath the sleep-coverings, and her arm came free. With it, she flung the coverings off her body and promptly shrieked in terror.

For she saw that her own seal coverings and jewelry had since been removed. And on her bare chest were many strings, attached to her flesh by flat, round parasite mouths! Her midsection and right wrist were pinned with straps like the one she had broken free of, and, worst of all, from her snared forearm protruded a long, transparent thing like a worm, a lump where it burrowed beneath her skin!

"Ayaaaaa!"

Beep! Beep! Beep! Beep!

Snap!

She broke free of the other arm strap, rose up further, and, with both hands, tore the bigger strap from her stomach. Then she swung her legs over the side of this high rest, and her feet landed on a cool floor, made up of tiny squares. Around her in the chamber were objects. Rectangular objects, sides and surfaces meeting in sharp corners, and a pole, from which hung a pouch half-filled with fluid, a pouch that joined with the worm-thing in her arm.

She tugged gingerly at where the grotesquerie penetrated her flesh, peeling off some kind of sticky folds and extracting a head like a mosquito's, with a needle for a mouth. Blood trickled from her arm, and from the mouth came fluid, rather sweet-smelling. With a scream, she tossed it to the floor.

The bird chirped faster, faster. Where was it? Following the sound, she looked up to her right and saw not a bird...

...but a monster!

A beeping monster with a square head, a face like black ice, and, on this, a waving beam of light. From the monster's silver body came the strings, or tentacles, attached to her chest!

Beep! Beep! Beep! The monster chirped faster. The light on its face went straight up and down. The Toonijuk yanked at the tentacles. They popped right off. Then...

Beeeeeeeeeeeeeee!

...from the monster came this piercing whistle. The Toonijuk covered her ears, seeing the light beam as it stopped waving. Became a flat line.

Whimpering, the Toonijuk hopped off the thing she had laid upon, looking about for escape-way, but seeing only solid wall, except where the sunlight filtered through. Something about the light was wrong to her, but before she could think what, she heard a clicking and saw a slender object on the farthest wall turning. Then a rectangular section swung away from the rest, and into the chamber rushed two of the Naked.

Their eyes widened when they saw the Toonijuk, and they began making sounds. Harsh coughing gutturals. One waved and flapped his arms, the other tensed his body. The Toonijuk stepped backwards, observing that neither carried weapons and that the chamber entrance had not been resealed.

They jabbered and gibbered at each other, and the Toonijuk understood this to be a kind of Naked-speech. But it wasn't the speech of the Inuit, and these two were not of them, either. For these Naked had skin as white as the Beluga. One was thin, with almost no hair on his head, and the other was short and stocky, with long yellow hair. The thin one wore white coverings, and the short one wore all brown.

But they were still the Naked, with little ears and little mouths and lemming-beady eyes. They were killers. Murderers.

The Toonijuk bellowed. Bared her teeth.

The thin Naked shook and hopped away like the frightened hare, but the other stayed his ground, watching the Toonijuk like the sentry Wolf. She smelled no fear in him. He made hushed sounds and held up a hand. Directing speech at her, the Toonijuk realized. Her eyes darted to the open chamber entrance. Still speaking, Yellow Hair stepped closer.

The Toonijuk bolted for the entrance.

Yellow Hair shouted and blocked her way. She skirted around him, but he lunged and grabbed her by the arm.

The Toonijuk growled. Swatted the Naked.

Her open hand met his chest, knocking Yellow Hair off her and to the floor. The Toonijuk ran out of the chamber...

...and found herself racing down a tunnel just as white-walled and square-edged. Weird, glowing strips of light above. Behind her, footfalls. The Naked, giving pursuit.

The Toonijuk ran, ran, then stopped.

The tunnel diverged into two, one going directly left, the other right. Which way? Which way? The Toonijuk looked back and saw the Naked, only a few paces away, like the Weasel on the Vole's trail.

Thinking no further, she went left.

This tunnel was arched, wider than the last and more-dimly lit. It sloped downwards, the lighting growing less and less until the Toonijuk found herself in total blackness, her sight gone. She stopped, before she ran into a wall, and listened. The pursuit must have ended for no Naked moved bear-soundlessly. Here in the dark she might hide and even escape. Sniffing, the Toonijuk proceeded ahead cautiously. The tunnel had become damp. She heard dripping, and her feet landed in puddles. The air was so humid and hot! Where was she? Some kind of Naked-dwelling, she guessed, but much larger than the dwellings this one had ever seen!

She pressed on, looking desperately about for light and an escape-way. Kept thinking about the tentacled monster and worm that had been violating her flesh. What evil had the Naked done to her shell? And where was??

There was a noise, a clanging, somewhere ahead. The Toonijuk stopped.

A cool draft hit her, and she winced at a grim stench, like caribou spat and rotting flesh. Growing stronger. She heard a

Thump! Thump! Thump!

Loud footfalls. Too loud for the Naked.

They stopped, and the Toonijuk next heard sniffing. Followed by...

...a roar!

Like many of the Bear, echoing through the tunnel. Then footfalls again. Running. The Toonijuk turned and ran herself.

The footfalls became louder. Gaining. But as the Toonijuk began to race upslope and the light returned, they stopped, and behind her the Toonijuk heard what sounded like laughter.

She was back at the crossways. There was Yellow Hair, still in the tunnel leading from the chamber where she had awakened, but now holding a death-spear!

The Toonijuk darted straight ahead, up the remaining un-traveled tunnel.

It was well lit, with walls of protruding rock.

It was also a short tunnel, ending in a wall of flat silver. The Toonijuk crashed against it, screaming and crying.

The Naked joined her in the tunnel, approaching stealthily, as the Wolf does the bull Musk Ox. The Toonijuk growled and bellowed, but the sight of that death-spear made her shake and spill body-water on the floor.

But Yellow Hair didn't aim it at her. Instead, he muttered into a small object that he held against mouth and ear. Nodding his head, Yellow Hair walked over to the tunnel wall and laid a hand on a protruding piece of gray. The Toonijuk heard a purring, and glanced behind her to see the blocking wall lifting like an eyelid. Disappearing into the ceiling. Revealing the brightness of day.

Yellow Hair barked at her and waved, as if signing for this one to go through the opening.

Strange. The Toonijuk sensed deceit. Yet...

She looked at the death-spear.

And ran. Outside.

Into daylight. Onto earth. Onto green.

Hearing and seeing no pursuit, but noticing how wrong the sun was. Low. Over the west horizon?! Made no sense!

And what was around her? Things. Big things sticking on the earth, like the hoofs and legs of a herd of giant caribou.

What?

Still running, the Toonijuk gazed up at something like fur, but green and...

Smack!

She went down, landing on a mat of dry, brittle needles. Spots danced before her eyes, and when they cleared, the Toonijuk saw clearly the thing she'd run into. A thing of red-brown scales topped with green fur. One of the monsters around her. A scream built in her throat...

...and quickly died for, rising, she saw that this life-form was not a monster at all.

It was... a plant!

She approached cautiously, touching the massive stem, looking up at the needled-greens, judging these plants as tall as a whale was long. Maybe even two whale.

"Karunk!"

So pretty! And their scent, as fragrant as a meadow in spring. The structure, the Toonijuk noted, was much like the "wood" from which the Inuit crafted their dwellings. But the sight brought to mind something else. Stories told her by the Shaman of how the Toonijuk had long ago lived in a land where the flowers touched the sky. A land of...

There was a sound, like coughing, behind her.

Whipping around, she saw a dark figure, standing only a pace away, pointing to the plants. Making obscene gutturals.

The Toonijuk ran.

Soon clearing the giants...

...and stopping, before she plunged off a cliff.

The Toonijuk stood on a rocky outcropping, looking down at a drop she could not survive. Ending in water. A body of water as wide as a Northland fiord. And on the other side and all around her she saw green and green and green. The tops of these giant plants. And beyond that, jagged, snowy peaks, higher than anything in the Toonijuk's homeground. She wondered, for the first time, if that death-spear had claimed her life, and now her Spirit walked the Sky-Ground. But why should it go there?

Unfamiliar bird of blue, gray, and white flew by. There was a splash, and her gaze caught way below an upright form, huge and black, bounding out of the water onto the rocky shore, quickly vanishing into the surrounding vegetation.

Behind her, light footfalls and a guttural. She turned to see the dark figure that had frightened her a moment ago now joining her on the ledge. She tensed for flight... or struggle.

But it moved not as if to attack, but at a slow amble, carrying a brown-wrapped bundle under one arm. In the open light, the Toonijuk got a better look at its coverings, a cloak and hood, the last of which cast the face in shadow. Both made of what seemed black fish-skin, yet as the sun hit them, they flickered and shined as the Gods did when they showed themselves in the night sky.

Grunting, gurgling, the figure stepped closer to the Toonijuk and, with a scaly hand, removed the hood.

The Toonijuk gasped...

...for the head was dusky blue and walrus-lumpy, with a main of spiky black hair. The nose was flat and upturned, and the mouth as wide as the Wolf's!

The monster grinned.

And the Toonijuk shrieked, seeing many sharp teeth.

A demon!

She understood.

Understood her spirit wandered not the Sky-Grounds, but Lokk, as it should wander, and this was Navra herself, come to punish her!

But then the demon spoke.

Spoke with a raspy but masculine voice as it pointed around at the fantastic plants. Repeating a sound, slower and slower, until the Toonijuk heard,

"Treeees."

He stepped closer. The Toonijuk slapped her chest. Bellowed.

"Keep from! Keep from this Toonijuk!"

The demon cocked his head. Said,

"Toonijuk?"

He withdrew a few lengths, all the while making speech. But this time not guttural, but melodious and ear-pleasing, filled with whistles and clicks. Much like Toonijuk. But this one still couldn't understand.

He bent over, setting the bundle down, unwrapping it.

And again the Toonijuk gasped...

...as she saw the walrus tusk, her walrus tusk, with its black squiggly markings. The demon held it up, making sounds. Then...

"What?" asked the Toonijuk.

Certain she heard, among those sounds, "Totem of this one?"

The demon gently set the tusk on the wrappings and backed away, waving his hand in a circle and pointing to the ground, like one Toonijuk would do to another, telling them it was safe to approach.

The demon stopped at the where the giant plants stood, speaking in a tongue so much like Toonijuk. Placing two clenched hands on his chest, a gesture very much like the Toonijuk hand-sign meaning "Show no fear."

He then sat on the ground, cross-legged, holding up both hands. This was what Toonijuk did when strangers approached their camp.

This one stayed where she was, well fearing Raven-deceit. One could not trust a demon! But still, the Totem belonged to her. To her Clan. She must reclaim it.

Seeing a large stone, she picked it up. Brandished it at the demon, who merely nodded, as with approval.

The Toonijuk slowly approached. The demon sat unmoving. Silent.

The Toonijuk got to the tusk. Bent down, still brandishing the stone, not taking her sight from that terrible creature, from its horrible face, and...

...the eyes!

Wide and light gray. Gentle?

Toonijuk eyes.

No. Whatever this beast might be, it was not Toonijuk. But neither was he the Naked.

She grabbed the tusk. Cradled it against her chest.

He spoke. Voice low, soothing.

The Toonijuk realized she was crying because she had feared the Clan-Totem lost. Why should a demon return it?

He continued to speak, and the Toonijuk looked into those eyes, so much like her own, hearing a word that sounded so much like Toonijuk. So much like,

"Friend."

Sweet Blood

Gary Bolstridge

*W*e are what we eat. Even we, the living dead, are finding it increasingly difficult to locate a good meal. We do not eat a variety of food, but we do take in the composition of our victims' blood, so we must choose carefully. As the world becomes more sophisticated, ethnic culinary delights are finding their way into all cultures. Unusual restaurants are cropping up right around the neighborhood corner. The average person is able to experience a wide sample of rich and exotic foods, which translates directly to their blood. These foods cause individuals to vary in taste.

It wasn't always like this. While big cities have a variety of choices, the countryside is simple and stable. Rural folk can be counted on for hardy meals. Their blood, less contaminated with chemicals and unknown flavors, is more consistent, reliable and satisfying. They have a saying: the more time you spend on this earth, the more you appreciate the simple things.

"I'll have a triple Café Mocha, Venti, please." I know it is bad for me, but I've decided to indulge myself, which is a good thing once in a while. It isn't the espresso that does the damage (though I definitely get the caffeine jitters); the sugar is the killer. My body is cursed. Whatever sugar I take in remains unprocessed in my blood. But my numbers have been good for the past month, rarely going above the danger zone of 120. In fact, it was 95 mg/dL when I woke up, and I need something to get me going. Especially since I had to get moving for work in the cold before sunrise.

I remove the lid from the cup and add cinnamon on top of the whipped cream. Using a coffee stirrer, I ladle the tasty layer into my mouth. Actually, this is the best part of the drink. I continue until all of the whipped cream is gone and add more cinnamon to the remaining brew. My doctor might think this is a little over the edge, but Hey, you only live once!

I take a sip, and an "Ummmm" involuntarily escapes my throat. I quickly look around the room to see if anyone noticed my utterance. Everyone seated in the coffee shop is reading newspapers or talking to each other. The people in line are staring impatiently at the girl behind the counter.

As I gaze toward my sweet concoction, my eye happens to look through the window, and I see a man staring directly at me. I know he couldn't have heard me, so I decide not to give it any further thought.

I walk out of the coffee shop and take another sip of my brew. Yeah, it tastes good. I long ago weaned myself off sweet things, but the taste of the chocolate more than justifies my indulgence. My mind goes into a temporary relaxation. It is only a matter of time before the sugar and caffeine change that. I am enjoying the moment.

I stop to look in a shop window when I notice a faint earthy odor. It has an undertone of decay to it, but also a pleasant woody high note and a strong smell of moss. Breathing it in, I become a little light-headed, so I jump when I look to my side and see the man from outside the coffee bar standing nearby. I didn't hear his approach. He turns in my direction and smiles, revealing perfect teeth. I nod toward him, turn, and walk away.

I continue to stroll at a leisurely pace, sipping my mocha. My head clears as the strong odor dissipates. I cast an occasional glance behind me. The stranger keeps pace at a discreet distance. Even in the darkness just before sunrise, I can see him. I realize I am being followed.

Having another man follow you on a nearly deserted street this early in the morning becomes disconcerting when you haven't done anything to provoke contact. It can be a creepy sort of compliment... it can even be hazardous to your health. Not that I'm inclined to that sort of activity; there isn't any chance of that from me. But you never know what someone else has in mind.

He isn't very subtle about stalking me. In fact, he is rather cavalier, with a self-confidence that bothers me a great deal. I consider letting him catch up so I can reject him, but he isn't afraid of being found out. As if I could do him any harm. Because we are in public, I determine that I'm not in much danger, so I continue my stroll.

I had my eye on a particular victim. He looked innocuous enough, promising a stable meal that would keep me from waking up hungry in the middle of the day. Having seen him in the coffee shop, I knew I was in for a special treat.

I needed to confirm a few things, however, and decided to follow him. After many lifetimes' experience, I have come to a few conclusions that mortal doctors have only recently begun to appreciate: I have learned that blood directly reflects a person's habits.

Blood is a very revealing medium in humans. It carries diseased cells, which have an unappealing taste, but we are immune to disease. It transfers sugar from foods, giving the body energy while retaining distinct flavors. For instance, the blood of Italians and Greeks is disagreeable because they flavor most of their food with garlic — and every schoolboy knows the effects of garlic.

We are able to ingest animal blood, but the taste of grass and hay is hardly appetizing. Carnivorous animals are becoming increasingly difficult to find. And you can't play the mental games with them that you can with humans. There's the real challenge.

One thing in his favor — he did not smoke. Tobacco tends to give blood an acrid taste that is not very appealing. There are other traits I have observed.

Never prey on a politician; telling lies really is in their blood.

The blood of an actor induces a strong desire for recognition, and it is bad for me to stand out.

Modern philosophers, on the other hand, cause you to question everything, resulting in inaction.

Similarly, the blood of a teacher results in complacency, from having to recite the same information repeatedly. It is the hunt that drives me.

Poets' blood is rich, literally, with emotion, but it is a bit syrupy and thick, hard to digest, hard to swallow, making it difficult to take.

Writers' blood is thin and watery, not enough depth.

Artists have a lot of imagination but also a lot of confusion; they worry too much. They need to make a mark for themselves and are always trying things without conviction. The last thing I need is to question purpose. It becomes difficult to track future victims.

Some of my kind seek out drug addicts; they like the high.

Teenage girls are too emotional, up and down, causing vacillating indecision. I get confused and jittery. I lose my train of thought; my powers are diminished. This is why it is better to choose an adult male victim, less variable.

Teenage boys are not good victims. Too much testosterone in their blood — they also make me edgy and nervous. I do not need to take chances.

Taking the time to choose meals with care helps to break the tedium of living for so long. One thing I have in my favor is time. Patience and observation have served me well.

This one was walking slowly, he obviously noticed me following him. He felt secure for the moment, but given time everyone makes a mistake — a fatal mistake.

I continue to walk, drinking my half-finished coffee. I no longer look into shop windows when I stop. I look behind me to see if I am still being followed.

The clouds part, releasing captive moonlight, and I can clearly see him. His skin is translucent like fine alabaster, but lacking its warm red glow. Instead, blue and green veins insinuate themselves, barely visible. His lips are close to being red, but more of a burgundy color, as when a red rose has gone past its bloom and begun to fade into death.

The gap between us seems to be lessening. The rotted decaying odor increases from time to time. The air chills when he is near. Just as I realize that he is the source, my mind becomes confused, and I start to lose direction. Then a strong, crisp wind blows, clearing my head.

The cup of coffee in my hand becomes heavy, and I almost drop it a few times when he is near. The confusion caused by the odor is cumulative, and each breeze has less of a clearing effect on my mind. Whenever I get a jolt from the caffeine and sugar, his presence neutralizes it. I feel the sugar building up in my system, rushing along with my blood.

I find myself wandering off the main walk, not realizing why. I'm hearing thoughts that aren't mine. Can a person think in a language they are unable to speak? In tongues that time has silenced, and know they are languages that nobody alive has ever heard? Meanings are universal, through time and language, carrying the same content from man's earliest beginnings. Deep down I know these thoughts, experienced by countless others before me, are false. They have sinister connotations. I can also hear voices crying out to me to take care, to resist. Resist what? I don't have a clue.

He was weakening, his mind becoming supple, his will virtually non-existent. It is at this point that I am able to determine if a man is worthy of a meal. He seemed plain enough, dressed in denim jeans — the uniform of blandness. He wore a lot of jewelry, including bracelets, implying a layer of vanity.

People's diets are reflected in their appearances. This one seemed to enjoy simple food but liked to accessorize — adding highlights of flavor. A plain base allows each additional individual flavor to be tasted and savored. He relished flavor. As do I.

I am in a part of the city where I have never been before. The shadows are my friends, my confidantes. He is close, very close — I can feel it. I involuntarily drop the empty coffee cup to the dry brown leaves at my feet. I am no longer alarmed by his presence; he fills my mind. The image of him has faded, his flesh forgotten. I remember only the color of his lips. I need to see him, to talk to him. I turn a corner to wait for him.

I stood next to him, sensing his warm skin. He moved toward me, and I instantly attacked his neck. A surprising "Ummmm" involuntarily escaped my throat. I quickly looked around to see if anyone had noticed my utterance. Confirming we were unobserved, I continued to enjoy my dessert. He tasted sweet and sugary, more so than a normal human. Suddenly, I could feel the chocolate and caffeine jolt through my system, from his veins into mine. Too late, I realized my mistake.

Unable to rest, I've been lying awake in my coffin well into the morning, staring at the wood grain patterns on the lid.

Damn diabetics.

from A Circle of Two: Book of Newport

A. Valentine Smith

An Equal and Opposite Magikal Reaction

School was out, and the girls were again walking home. The sky was a bit overcast, but the air was warm. Sandy and April were looking forward to a rare night without homework.

"You'll never believe what I saw the other day, Sandy."

"What?" Sandy was having problems concentrating on April's words. Instead, she was thinking about what they could do on their free night.

"Mandy asked Vaughn to the dance!" April piped up brightly.

"Oh, really? Shouldn't Vaughn have asked Mandy?"

"This is the Twenty First Century. So when did you become so old fashioned?" April retorted.

"Whatcha got there?" Sandy pointed to April's arm.

"Got bored during lunch. Got a little vine and this flower from the school gardener. I wove it into a bracelet," April said matter-of-factly.

She looked down at her wrist to where the beach rose flower dangled from her crude bracelet.

Good thing he gave me a vine from a different plant, April thought. The beach rose stems were thorny and too inflexible for a bracelet. April hadn't made the bracelet loop small enough, and it kept slipping down her forearm toward her elbow or off of her wrist, depending on how she held her arm.

Both girls heard someone running behind them. They turned to see Mandy trying to catch up to them. When Mandy finally caught up, she was totally out of breath.

"Mandy, what happened?" Sandy asked.

"Missed the bus," Mandy puffed between breaths. "Thought I'd walk home with you."

"Sure, but you're like a mile beyond my house," April answered.

"No problem. My mom will give you a ride," Sandy volunteered. The girls walked on in silence for a couple of minutes.

"Speaking of rides, I've got my driver's permit. If I can get my older sister to come along, do you want to catch a movie tonight?" Mandy asked.

April and Sandy suddenly look up and stop dead in their tracks. Mandy isn't able to react as quickly and collides with the two girls.

"What the heck's wrong with you two?" a flustered Mandy blurts.

Sandy and April ignore her. They're staring at a weird pulsating glow coming from a patch of grass near the tree line.

"Do you see what I see?" Sandy asks.

April rubs her eyes. The glow seems so surreal. Both girls slowly approach the glow with Mandy in tow. Mandy's expression is extremely quizzical.

"What are you looking at? You guys aren't weirding out on me, are you?" Mandy asks. She's starting to get worried.

Sandy and April kneel down around the glowing mass in the lump of grass. Poor Mandy can only hunch over them with no clue as to what they're doing. April rubs her eyes again. She is the first to identify what they are looking at and how they see it.

"It's a black crystal," April says. "And I think I know why we can see it." April looks at Sandy knowingly. All of a sudden Sandy catches on.

"Seventh Sight," Sandy blurts.

"What are you guys babbling about?" Mandy looks from one girl to the other.

"Aunt Penny said to use our 'Seventh Sight' to see the 'Seeds of Evil,'" Sandy says. She tries hard to remember what Aunt Penny had said about the outcomes of the Seeds of Evil. Aunt Penny had also said that she and

April needed to do something, but Sandy can't remember. She slowly looks up into the trees above, where sounds of chirping birds are coming from.

That looks like the mother bird from the time April and I saved the baby bird, she thinks. It sounds like mother bird is shrilling a warning.

"Aunt Penny said?... What do you mean? She passed away." April is unaware of Sandy's dream visit with Penny. April's attention is diverted back to the clump of grass. She stares at the crystal and appears to be mesmerized. A hypnotic cobra couldn't have done a better job of luring April into a trance than the glowing black crystal is doing. Her hand slowly reaches out toward the Evil beauty.

Sandy is mumbling to herself. "Seeds... outcome... Seeds... outcome," she keeps chanting. Then it hits her all at once. "Rule #2: For every good Magikal Spell there is an equal but opposite Evil potential!" Sandy shouts. Mandy jumps back in surprise from this outburst.

The Seed of Evil is the result of cheating death. Sandy is trying to think fast. If she can't remember Aunt Penny's words, maybe she can think through this. Something is very important. She has to remember.

Her train of thought is broken when she catches sight of April's hand extending toward the dark crystal.

"No!" Sandy screams, but it's too late. April touches the crystal, and the dark glow immediately shoots up her arm, almost to her shoulder.

She recoils in agony, too stunned to cry out. Her bracelet breaks, and the beach rose flower disintegrates, showering the air with red petals. April collapses.

A Circle of Two: Book of Newport
by A. Valentine Smith
(Xlibris, 2001)

Available in hard cover and paperback from Waldenbooks, Bellevue Ave., Newport, RI, Amazon, Barnes and Noble (BN.com), SamGoody.com, BooksaMillion (BAMM.com), Walmart.com, and by special order. E-book available from the publisher at www.xlibris.com. More information at www.alientimetreasure.com.

Life Grows Richer Still

Ingrid Mathews

Morning's early sunlight beckons
Toward its effervescent rays
To a place of tranquil beauty
Bathed in misty morning gray

To a wood of stately statues
Having endured the test of time
Forming a magnificent cathedral
Reaching for the cerulean sky

Angled light casts lengthy shadows
Unique and perfect, a paradigm set
Much like soldiers at attention
Waiting for orders to forge ahead

Now in peaceful wood I stand alone
Among these gently swaying giants
Listening to the leaves above me
Dancing in the awakening breeze

I long to know what woods these are
Which welcome me with sanguine arms
Embracing me like a long lost lover
Not wanting to let go

In its warm and reticent grip
I sense life's ephemeral breath
And can't help feeling all the while
Life grow richer still

Ingrid Mathews